T0305878

Personnel Administration in an Automated Environment

Personnel Administration in an Automated Environment

Philip E. Leinbach
Editor

Routledge
Taylor & Francis Group

NEW YORK AND LONDON

Personnel Administration in an Automated Environment has also been published as *Journal of Library Administration,* Volume 13, Numbers 1/2.

First Published 1990 by The Haworth Press, Inc.

Published 2013 by Routledge
605 Third Avenue, New York, NY 10017
4 Park Square, Milton Park, Abingdon, Oxon OX14 4RN

Routledge is an imprint of the Taylor & Francis Group, an informa business

Copyright © 1990 Taylor & Francis

Library of Congress Cataloging-in-Publication Data

Personnel administration in an automated environment / Philip E. Leinbach.
     p.   cm.
    "Has also been published as Journal of Library Administration, volume 13, numbers 1/2, 1990" —T.p. verso.
    Includes bibliographical references.
    ISBN 1-56024-032-6 (alk. paper)
    1. Library personnel management —Data processing. 2. Library administration —Data processing. 3. Libraries—Automation—Management —Data processing. I. Leinbach, Philip E.
Z682.P393 1990
023'.0285 —dc20
                                        90-39450
                                              CIP

ISBN 13: 978-1-56024-032-7 (hbk)

Personnel Administration
in an Automated Environment

CONTENTS

ABOUT THE EDITOR

Philip E. Leinbach, MLS, is University Librarian at Tulane University in New Orleans, Louisiana. As the university librarian, he has managed the installation of an online integrated library system along with other computer-based operations at the Tulane library. He worked in acquisitions and serials at Harvard University Library and later became Assistant University Librarian for Personnel there. Mr. Leinbach is an active member of the American Library Association, having served on the Advisory Committee for the Office of Library Personnel Resources, the Committee on Pay Equity, and the Committee on the Status of Women in Librarianship. He has also published articles on continuing education and library salaries.

Introduction

Computer technology has come to all but the smallest of American libraries. Some libraries have over twenty-five years of experience in coping with computers. The sophistication of many of our computer-based systems is truly remarkable, as computers become more mind-like. Nevertheless, computers are only tools, still to be used by human beings — who have yet to change to the extent of the tools. And as long as people are involved, there are personnel issues.

This special collection focuses on the effects of computer applications on selected facets of personnel administration in libraries. Some writers analyze the changes already wrought; others, with the changes happening today; and still others with changes likely in the future. But whatever the time frame, it is clear that all authors agree that automation has significant impact on the library workplace.

Library educator Kathleen M. Heim and two of her colleagues take a fresh look at the education of library automation personnel. Expanding on her article in this book, Dean Heim lays out a specific curriculum for the library systems analyst, pointing out the necessity for strong links with other university departments. The authors make a persuasive case for centering continuing education for automation specialists in the library schools. Although many schools are rising to the occasion, there are "enduring problems" in training the needed specialists — notably low salaries for the graduates and obtaining qualified faculty and sufficient resources. As small and mid-sized libraries increasingly hire automation librarians, recruiting them will be a growing personnel issue.

Supporting the observations of the LSU writers on salaries for automation librarians is the research of John Budd, author of several previous articles on librarians' salaries. Budd analyzes recent advertisements for comparative data on minimum salaries and required qualifications. Not surprisingly, he finds that the practice of paying automation librarians more than other types of librarians continues, creating morale problems, in some cases. It is simply a question of supply and demand. On the other hand, salaries in other professions requiring computer science education are clearly higher than in librarianship. Still, most employers require experience or education in library work, thus limiting the pool to those already in a relatively low-salaried market. Thus, Budd posits that existing salaries are a definite limitation to the supply of automation librarians.

Jennifer Cargill has published books and articles on a wide variety of library topics but is probably best known for her work on technical services activities. For this volume she looks at the impact of technology on all staff but her focus is clearly on information services staff. She sees technological change giving libraries tremendous opportunities for new services, which she speculates on in detail. In turn, new services will recast old organizational issues and raise some new ones, which will, in turn, bring forth new staff issues. Her conclusion is that libraries which fail to take advantage of the opportunities made possible by the Information Age will become "backwater libraries." A source list of materials on the change process and the impact of technology on staff should prove very useful.

Ann Prentice, who describes herself as in a position involving the "management of technology in a constantly changing environment," reminds us that planning and training are the key elements in managing change. She gives an excellent analysis of the impact of technology on the workforce and the workplace, applying the general principles to the library environment. She exhorts us to be the leaders in defining information jobs, for, like Cargill, she does not want us to miss a ripe opportunity.

What personnel issues *are* raised when new service initiatives based on computer technology are taken? Danuta Nitecki gives us some answers in her paper describing two projects at the University of Maryland at College Park Library. In the first instance, two groups of reference librarians were asked to design a simple expert system using a commercially available shell. In the second project, reference librarians, using the same expert system, acted as consultants to users organizing their own information sources. Very practical lessons in managing time and resources and the restructuring of traditional tasks such as the reference interview and user instruction were learned. Nitecki believes firmly that reference libraries can and must be involved in microcomputer software applications for handling users' information needs.

Drawing on a number of years of academic library reference experience, Cecilia D. Stafford and William M. Serban also deal with the changing nature of the front-line, reference desk librarian. Here is a commonsense, step-by-step approach to building a successful reference department in today's computer-based environment. They take us from analyzing the department's needs, to recruiting and training, to performance evaluation. The identification of six core competencies needed by the reference librarian brings Danuta Nitecki's work in 1983 up to date.

Lewis D. Cartee, Jr., poses three questions to probe the issue of whether automation is producing a new kind of manager. In being forced to deal with these questions as they apply to fiscal management, human resources management, organizational structure, decision making, and leadership, Cartee finds that, indeed, both the role and characteristics of successful library managers are changing. He reminds us that technological innovations mean an unstable, unpredictable environment *demanding* a new kind of manager. He believes that creative solutions to library issues are more needed than ever.

For many library managers, a totally new issue that has emerged since the introduction of computers is the relationship between the library and the computer facility. In fact, in recent years on many campuses, the question has become one of possible merger. Donald Waters brings to our discussion a background of experience in both the campus computing organization and the library. He describes the structural relationships that have emerged, concluding that the distance between the two has definitely narrowed in the last few years. Observing that total mergers will be rare, he sees partnership as the most likely successful form. A systematic, commonly-understood framework must be developed so that the "task arenas" can be identified. Waters proposes one that succinctly shows where the interests of the library and the campus intersect.

Two of our authors write from a technical services viewpoint, although both emphasize their belief in the general applicability of their conclusions. Elizabeth Dickinson Nichols, using her public library experiences, details the human and organizational impacts of automation, disagreeing with the prevalent view that computerization results in "isolated, robot-like staff." Instead, she finds an encouragement of "versatile, creative, people-oriented, 'renaissance' workers." Job content for all levels of staff change – a positive development, in her view.

Darla H. Rushing reports on the automated environment's effect on staffing patterns, on issues such as territoriality, and on future staffing in seven medium-sized academic libraries. Libraries of this type and size struggle to find the staff resources to automate (rarely is there a full-time systems librarian), yet are expected by users, particularly faculty, to offer the computer-based services of the ARL-size libraries. Technical services staff can rarely be reduced – in fact, catalog maintenance is requiring, in many cases, *more* staff.

Using a self-administered questionnaire and an interview, Leigh Estabrook and two colleagues at the University of Illinois at Urbana-Champaign, examined the level of job satisfaction of both librarians and support staff in four academic libraries. Her purpose was to find out if automation made a difference in worker satisfaction. While many support staff expressed a liking for working with computers, Estabrook concludes that automation has little effect on job satisfaction. Instead, the oft-cited needs for "control, independence, and social interaction" lead to a satisfied worker. However, these qualities of worklife could be highly impacted by organizational change, which automation *does* appear to be affecting. Thus, she cautions us to pay attention to the psychological and social needs of the staff as we go through automation-induced reorganizations.

Geraldine B. King takes us through the steps of creating or adapting a performance appraisal system. While many factors have remained the same, the automated environment has produced new conditions which must be taken into account in evaluating staff performance.

Several of our authors have provided bibliographies for those wanting to do additional reading. Margaret Myers of the ALA Office for Library Personnel Resources has compiled a general one on library automation and personnel issues. Selected and annotated, her list is an excellent guide to the topic.

Philip E. Leinbach

Educating for Automation:
Can the Library Schools Do the Job?

John P. McLain
Danny P. Wallace
Kathleen M. Heim

INTRODUCTION

The proliferation of computers in today's society has caused an increased demand for individuals capable of effectively dealing with both computers and people, and the library environment is no exception. The skills of these intermediaries, dictated by the diverse milieus they must traverse, will have to be broad and somewhat deep. There are several possible ways of producing the technically trained individuals who are required. Perhaps the best method is to recruit individuals with a sound background in computer operations, and provide them with the professional education required for them to become librarians. This solution, however, does not seem likely on a large scale. It is unreasonable to expect such persons to spend an additional year in graduate school for library education when an automation position in a library will probably pay them twenty percent less than they could hope to make using only their technically oriented undergraduate degrees.[1]

Another alternative is to induce people who currently have library and information science degrees to pursue an advanced degree with an emphasis on library automation. This has been implemented with some success in some institutions,[2] but whether it can act as a viable alternative on a large scale is uncertain. Yet another

John P. McLain is Computer Resources Coordinator, Danny P. Wallace is Associate Professor, and Kathleen M. Heim is Dean, School of Library and Information Science, Louisiana State University, Baton Rouge.

alternative involves recruiting persons who have already chosen the library profession as their careers, and teaching them to be automation specialists as part of their basic professional education. A few library schools have attempted to design and implement some type of curriculum that will produce persons capable of filling these automation positions. These efforts, however, have only occurred on a very small scale, and are not very grandiose.

EDUCATING FOR AUTOMATION: BASIC NEEDS

Deerwester has suggested four levels of automation skills necessary in libraries, and the associated level of expertise an individual should possess to successfully operate at each level.[3] These are (1) the "general librarian," who will need a minimum amount of computer literacy to understand (and effectively exploit) the computer's role in the library environment; (2) the "librarian with technical responsibilities," who should be able to assess technical problems in the library environment and determine how they might be solved using a computer; (3) the "technical expert with library responsibilities," who has the skills present at the preceding level, but has a deeper understanding of computers and software, and of what can be accomplished with each; and finally (4) the "technical expert," who will have technical expertise at least comparable to that required by a bachelor's or maybe a master's degree in computer science or a closely related discipline.

Any change in information technology will inevitably be reflected in the curricular offerings of institutions that provide professional education for the library and information professions. According to Buckland, library and information technology will be the area of greatest change in library and information science education in the next century.[4] Past developments in areas such as microforms and current changes related to preservation of library materials are prominent examples of this effect, but perhaps no technological change since the invention of printing has had so sweeping an impact on libraries as has automation.

It is clear that schools of library and information science are making some attempt to provide educational experiences related to automation. A rather cursory examination of the currently available bulletins for ALA-accredited schools indicates that from two to twenty-two courses are offered that in some way emphasize the use of computers, with an overall average of nine such courses. The nature and difficulty of these courses varies substantially: there are courses that provide basic computer literacy on about the level currently being offered by many elementary schools, courses that emphasize the use of computers for library-oriented tasks such as working with bibliographic utilities or searching commercial database systems, courses that teach fairly sophisticated programming skills, and a very wide variety of other computer-oriented courses. Some of these courses are directly applicable to the education of library automation specialists, while others are clearly intended to impart those general automation skills and techniques required of non-specialists. Many of the courses may devolve as much from the desire of a particular instructor to teach a favorite topic as from a structured program of instruction, and in some cases the relationship between the course and the curriculum is less than apparent.

A SUGGESTED CURRICULUM FOR EDUCATING LIBRARY AUTOMATION SPECIALISTS

Suggesting specific courses of action for attaining a broad goal such as the education of library automation specialists is subject to the limitations of all philosophical statements aimed at improving instruction. Even when educators agree on the wisdom of a course of action, their ability to follow it is necessarily constrained by the resources of individual schools. It is possible, however, to speculate about an "ideal" graduate library and information science curriculum that addresses at least the first three levels of automation capabilities suggested above. This curriculum, consisting of twelve courses, is specifically oriented towards producing individuals qualified for level 3 of Deerwester's hierarchy. Individuals capable of operating at levels 1 and 2 can be educated using the same curriculum simply by using an appropriately selected subset of the curriculum.

The first four courses contain material that is standard in most library and information science programs and required in many. These "core" courses are not necessarily technology-oriented, are taken by all students in the program, and once completed, should have provided the participants with a basic knowledge of librarianship. Grover has suggested that at the conclusion of these core courses students should be able to (1) articulate a philosophy of the library and information professions; (2) recognize basic human behavior patterns applied to the communication of information; (3) comprehend the theory and general patterns of information transfer in society; (4) articulate the major methods of organizing information for use in the design and implementation of information systems; (5) manage an information system, employing appropriate management theory; (6) analyze information needs of a client group; (7) apply appropriate research methodologies and interpret research results in the management of an information system; (8) evaluate and design an information system, employing appropriate methods and technologies; and, (9) design appropriate services for a particular environment based on the comprehension of the societal functions of libraries and information centers (educational, cultural, informational, research, recreational, and bibliographic functions).[5] This is essentially a restatement in current terms of the traditional core of library and information science education, and the courses that cover this material are currently well established in all library schools. To be relevant to current needs, the mix of required courses must involve not only the traditional core of reference services, cataloging, collection development and management, but also some meaningful grounding in the use of current information technology. For the time being, this implies that students must leave the professional preparation program with the ability to use computer hardware and software to accomplish specific goals; that is, they must be computer literate in a way that relates effectively to the library and information system context.

In addition to the core courses required of all master's students, the following five courses, which are specifically designed to provide the student with a sound foundation of knowledge in library automation, are proposed to finish out the required curriculum for library automation specialists.

Advanced Microcomputers: This course is designed to give the student a thorough understanding of a disk operating system and the general hardware components of a microcomputer. Instructions on installing various hardware components (e.g., internal modems) and evaluation techniques for software selection are provided.

Statistical Inference: Basic concepts of statistical models and sampling are taught, as are various tests of hypotheses and estimation. Analysis of variance, correlation and regression are introduced and discussed. A general course in research methods for library and information science might act as a substitute for this course.

Analysis of Information Systems: Systems analysis techniques are applied to information systems, especially the design and implementation of more effective information processing and delivery systems. Skills learned in the two preceding courses are used for problem analysis/solving in this area.

Bibliographic Control Systems: Management and automation of library technical operations are presented. There is an emphasis on the evaluation, acquisition, and application of integrated automation systems in the library environment.

Practicum in Library Automation: The student applies the skills and techniques learned in the preceding courses in a real library environment. A real problem in an information center or library is researched and analyzed, and a solution is implemented with the student doing a major amount of the work in each step.

Although practica are common in library and information science programs, the notion of a practicum that emphasizes automation experiences appears to be new and may be from a planning and management perspective the most difficult part of the curriculum. It requires that automated systems be available or at least under development in the vicinity of the school, and also requires that faculty take a very active role in working with libraries to assure a meaningful experience for the practicum student. Some sort of supervised practical experience is essential if the student is to be adequately prepared to deal with a "real life" environment following graduation.

The common core and the required courses for automation specialists total nine courses. The remaining three courses of the twelve required for the degree are electives subject to student choice. These can be anything related to library and information science, but the most useful courses for a library automation student may include:

Management of Library Technical Services: Introduction to the nature and range of technical services in libraries, identification of technical services problems, analysis of technical services functions, and application of current management techniques and technology to technical operations.

Information Retrieval Systems: Discusses the current commercially available retrieval systems, query processing models, and current research problems.

Information Science: This course examines the theory, history, and philosophy of information science and information retrieval, with emphasis on the latter pertaining specifically to the library environment.

Database Management Systems: The three basic models of network, hierarchical, and relational database systems are discussed, as are the merits and disadvantages of each model.

Online Retrieval Systems: Intensive exposure to the use of commercially available online retrieval systems, including question negotiation, strategy development, tool selection and hands-on use of one or more systems.

Research Methods in Library and Information Science: This course brings together several of the courses above, such as Statistics and Operations Research, and directly relates them to the library environment.

Operations Research: The objective of the course is to teach the fundamentals of operations research, i.e., the determination of the best or optimum course of action for solving a problem under the restriction of limited resources. Topics such as queuing theory, inventory theory and simulation models are covered in this course.

Programming Languages: This course may be a general introduction to programming using one or more higher level languages for purposes of example or an intensive introduction to a single language. Use of a time sharing computer system is a highly desirable component.

To provide the student with such a diverse offering of courses, it may be necessary to go outside the school of library and information science. The necessary faculty expertise in all the above areas will seldom, if ever, be available within any one department. This argues for strong working ties with many other departments on campus, including areas such as statistics, computer science and business administration.

CONTINUING EDUCATION AND AUTOMATION

Although some sequence such as that described above may be optimal for the education of individuals entering the profession, another pressing need is that of providing further education for those already in professional positions. Continuing education can take multiple forms, including regular or special programs at professional conferences; nationally advertised workshops and institutes; locally based in-house workshops; short courses offered by schools of library and information science or other academic units; formal academic programs in library and information science or other pertinent fields; noncredit courses offered by universities, technical schools, public schools or businesses; correspondence courses, including those offered by professional associations; truly independent study through reading; and a myriad of other possibilities.

The commitment of librarians to continuing education is variable. Some librarians, such as those who seek to obtain and maintain certification as school or medical librarians, are virtually forced to engage in continuing education activities, and continuing education programs tailored to their needs are common. Other librarians may pursue continuing education on an occasional basis, pursuing options that are perhaps more informational than truly educational. Librarians in some environments, particularly academic librarians, may find it most beneficial to pursue further education in an area other than librarianship. Many librarians apparently pursue no deliberate course of continuing education, perhaps not even to the extent of attending conferences or maintaining awareness of the professional literature. Some seem to be actively opposed to learning anything new at any time or through any means.

Durrance has delineated five categories of continuing education programs related to advancing technology:

1. those that give librarians the desire to embrace a particular technological innovation . . .
2. programs that provide the knowledge or information necessary to become involved or to purchase the technology . . .
3. those programs that transmit the skills necessary to manipulate the technology . . .
4. CE offerings that provide specialized or advanced skills, and
5. programs that focus on the management skills necessary to oversee the technology.[6]

The needs of the automation specialist clearly exceed the first of Durrance's categories. Even programs that embrace the remaining four categories are not likely to provide true expertise. By implication and exclusion, Durrance has provided a pointer to a major problem with continuing education for library automation: those continuing education experiences most commonly pursued by librarians are probably not well suited to the professional development of library automation specialists.

To produce individuals capable of operating at level 4 of Deerwester's hierarchy, he suggests the individual obtain a second bachelor's or master's degree in computer science or a closely related area. It can take three to four years to accomplish the former, and one to three years to achieve the latter. Individuals already situated in the library work force will seldom be able to afford the time (and the expense of lost wages) in an effort to obtain either of these types of degrees. Although it might be possible to pursue such a degree on a part-time basis, doing so will delay completion of the degree considerably, and may put the student at risk of attaining a degree that is in part obsolete even before it is completed.

Furthermore, many — probably most — professional librarians simply don't have the necessary backgrounds for completing such degrees. Undergraduate programs in computer science tend to be highly competitive, and very high failure rates are common and in some cases apparently viewed as desirable. The typical librarian, with a limited quantitative and technical background and a full-time professional position to maintain, may find it very difficult to compete with well prepared, highly motivated undergraduates. Many master's degree programs assume a substantial undergraduate preparation, which means the librarian pursuing a master's degree in a computer-related area will probably have to make up those prerequisites before moving on to truly graduate level courses. Again, competition in the prerequisite courses may be problematic, and achievement of the master's degree will be delayed.

For most librarians who wish to gain technological expertise, then, the notion of pursuing either an undergraduate or graduate degree in computer science will represent a difficult, costly, long-term and ultimately undesirable course of action. Taking appropriate courses on a nondegree or noncredit basis might be an acceptable option for some, but the removal of the degree or course credit as a reward is typically not accompanied by any reduction in the demands of the courses, and the problem of being an adult professional in an undergraduate world remains. Other options include enrolling in adult education courses through public schools or private enterprises, but such courses are not likely to be reflective of the real needs of the library and information professions.

The most desirable form of continuing professional education for librarians is clearly some sort of program offered by a school of library and information science. For librarians who require an upgrade of their skills to the first or second levels of Deerwester's hierarchy, it may be possible to enroll in courses at a nearby school of library and information science on a nondegree basis. It will take an unusually well motivated librarian to pursue this course, however, and it will surely require that the individual be willing to invest in continuing education for the good of professional development and the good of the field, since it is unlikely that there will be other rewards.

Some kind of degree granting post-master's program seems likely to be the best course of action. A majority of ALA-accredited schools of library and information science do offer some sort of post-master's program short of the doctorate.[7] As Durrance has pointed out, however, post-master's certificate programs have "not become the primary method of delivery [for continuing education], comprising less than 1 percent of the degrees and less than 2 percent of the total library school enrollment."[8] Furthermore, the general mode of operation of post-master's certificate programs involves letting the student, presumably working with an advisor, pick and choose from existing library and information science courses to construct an individualized curriculum. Although this may work for schools that offer an appropriate mix of technology oriented courses, a more structured approach may be more desirable.

EXISTING PROGRAMS

It is clear that most schools of library and information science feel an obligation to address the need to provide students with some grounding in automation. Many institutions, including Rutgers[9] and Drexel[10] Universities, have recently made notable curriculum alterations in an attempt to meet this growing demand. An examination of the 1988 ALISE Statistical Report reveals that seventeen ALA-accredited schools added a total of twenty-five new automation-related courses during 1986-87.[11] Four schools reported that they have courses cross-listed with computer science departments, which suggests some emphasis on automation. Another emphasis is the existence of formalized joint degree programs involving library science and an automation-related discipline; two schools—the University of Hawaii at Manoa and Louisiana State University— offer such joint degree programs.[12] At other schools, the link to computer science is implied by the positioning of the library and information science program in the institution. The Pratt Institute, for instance, offers library and information science education through its School of Computer, Information and Library Sciences.

Other programs seem to be moving in directions that emphasize the broader scope of information services, often in conjunction with extensive attention to advancing technology, in a manner that de-emphasizes and in some cases appears to virtually ignore librarianship. The development of undergraduate and graduate programs in information science, information resources management, information technology and related areas is a valid response to a real need, but meeting the automation needs of libraries requires a program emphasizing both the "traditional" elements of librarianship and the operational elements of automation.

Several post-master's certificate programs, including those at the University of California — Berkeley, the University of Wisconsin — Madison, Queens College, the University of Hawaii at Manoa and Louisiana State University, contain components specifically designed to provide a continuing education experience related to library automation. The LSU program is described as having been "designed to allow the experienced information professional an opportunity to refresh basic professional competencies or develop proficiency in an area of specialization."[13] The University of Hawaii program, described as being "intended to allow students to specialize in applying computer and information technologies to information environments and in determining information policy and planning strategies,"[14] appears to be oriented more toward information retrieval systems than library automation.

ENDURING PROBLEMS IN EDUCATING
FOR AUTOMATION

One of the most apparent problems in the education of library automation specialists is that of recruiting students. The optimal solution to producing qualified library system analysts is to locate individuals with the necessary technical background (and inclination) and teach them to be librarians. Unfortunately, this may also be the least feasible method on a large scale. Students with a bachelor's degree in computer science may well be able to demand salaries comparable to entry level salaries for librarians who have completed master's degrees, and will almost undoubtedly be able to enter career paths in which salary increases are frequent and substantial. If a well qualified individual does choose to earn a master's degree in library and information science, there is still a high probability that he or she "may be attracted by higher salary opportunities and thereby be co-opted by the second profession,"[15] and move on into a more lucrative career in business or industry. There is actually a very high potential for such individuals being co-opted by the library automation industry and seeking employment with one of the vendors of automated systems or as an independent consultant rather than in a library. There must be a greater parity in the salaries for individuals interested in the library profession if we are to continue to attract (and keep) qualified technical people. Similarly, the impetus for midcareer librarians to pursue an additional degree may be rather limited, given the poor reward structure common to libraries. Automation in libraries will continue to grow rapidly, but unless these problems are addressed by the libraries that employ automation specialists, it will too often be under the supervision of persons who are not completely qualified to supervise these transformations.

Another problem is that of developing appropriate interdepartmental relationships. Many of the joint degree programs currently in place in schools of library and information science "appear to be aimed mostly at enhancing the skills of librarians in special environments rather than using degrees in other disciplines to enhance the overall ability of the librarian as a librarian."[16] Such cooperative activities involve virtually no real or ongoing effort on the part of the school or its faculty, and are in some cases cooperative in name only. The development of meaningfully interdepartmental programs requires effort and commitment, and may require that library and information science educators learn to look at their environment in a wholly new way.

A third problem area involves attracting qualified faculty. There are few faculty members who are truly qualified to teach and advise in areas related to library automation. The most recent ALISE directory lists a substantial number of people who are interested in or teach in areas related to automation, data processing, and systems analysis,[17] but it is not clear that all those persons listed are truly possessed of the expertise needed to teach library automation specialists. The problems of attracting qualified faculty are very similar to those of attracting qualified students: (1) most library and information science educators come from careers as librarians, and have not had intensely technological educations; (2) individuals with technological backgrounds can be hired to serve on library and information science faculties, but may lack the library background necessary for effective teaching of library automation; and (3) finding individuals with both the technological and library background who are also competent teachers is a very difficult task indeed. Furthermore, providing meaningful education for automation specialists requires a substantial effort on the part of the school as a whole. Designating one faculty member as the school's library automation educator isn't likely to be enough.

A final problem area is that of providing adequate teaching facilities. As Schlesinger has pointed out, "at a time when other professional schools are setting up laboratories with a dozen microcomputers linked in a local area network, the facilities provided by some library schools are laughable."[18] Education for automation specialists inherently requires instruction in the use of up-to-date hardware and software. Although the needs of the first two levels of Deerwester's hierarchy may be met through a well-equipped microcomputer laboratory, the needs of levels 3 and 4 require at least an introduction to the use of large computers. In addition to the hardware and software, a useful microcomputer lab must have a staff of well prepared assistants to help students learn the use of the lab's facilities and solve the problems that are a daily part of such a lab environment. It is not even clear that most schools currently are capable of meeting even the basic needs of all library and information science students, and meeting the needs of future automation specialists may seriously strain the resources of many schools.

CONCLUSION

The working title suggested for this article by the issue editor was "Educating for Automation: Can the Library Schools Do the Job?" That title has been preserved, and the discussion above leads to this answer: "Yes, they can, if they work hard enough, develop interdisciplinary curricula, and are willing and able to allocate the necessary resources."

NOTES

1. Boyce, Bert R. and Kathleen M. Heim. "The Education of Library Systems Analysts for the Nineties." *Journal of Library Administrations* 9:4 (1988) : 69-76.

2. Wallace, Danny P. and Bert R. Boyce. "Computer Technology and Inter-

disciplinary Efforts: A Discussion and Model Program." *Journal of Education for Library and Information Science* 27:3 (Winter 1987) : 158-168.

3. Deerwester, Scott. "Teaching about Computers and Technology." *Bulletin of the American Society of Information Science* 12:4 (April/May 1986) : 8.

4. Michael Buckland, quoted in Holley, Edward G. "Does Library Education Have a Future?" *American Libraries* 17 (October 1986) : 706.

5. Grover, Robert J. "Library and Information Professional Education for the Learning Society: A Model Curriculum." *Journal of Education for Library and Information Science* 26:1 (Summer 1985) : 33-45.

6. Durrance, Joan C. "Library Schools and Continuing Professional Education: The De Facto Role and Factors That Influence It." *Library Trends* 34 (Spring 1986) : 683.

7. ALA does not accredit post-master's or doctoral degrees. For a listing of accredited schools offering post-master's degrees, see the current issue of *Graduate Library Education Programs Accredited by the American Library Association under Standards for Accreditation, 1972* (Chicago: American Library Association/COA, semi-annual).

8. Durrance, p. 688.

9. Anderson, James D., Belkin, Nicholas J., Lederman, Linda C., and Tefko Saracevic. "Information Science at Rutgers: Establishing New Interdisciplinary Connections." *Journal of the American Society for Information Science* 9:5 (September 1988) : 327-330.

10. Woodward, Diana. "Drexel University College of Information Studies: Evolving Programs, New Connections." *Journal of the American Society for Information Science* 39:5 (September 1988) 334-336.

11. *Library and Information Science Education Statistical Report 1988* (State College, PA: Association for Library and Information Science Education, 1988): 184-186.

12. *Ibid*, 155-156.

13. *Library Automation . . . A Growth Profession* (Baton Rouge: Louisiana State University School of Library and Information Science, March 1989): 12.

14. *1989-91 University of Hawaii at Manoa School of Library and Information Studies* (Honolulu: University of Hawaii at Manoa School of Library and Information Studies): 20.

15. Wallace and Boyce, p. 165.

16. Wallace and Boyce: p. 164.

17. *Journal of Education for Library and Information Science*, (Directory Issue 1987-88): 110-114.

18. Schlesinger, Louise D. "The View of the Student." In White, Herbert S., editor, *Education for Professional Librarians* (White Plains, NY: Knowledge Industry Publications, 1986): 243-244.

Salaries of Automation Librarians: Positions and Requirements

John M. Budd

In virtually every type of library managers are attempting to make the most of the opportunities and to solve the problems that accompany changes in technology. Over the past couple of decades these changes have been revolutionary. Librarians have dealt with alterations in concepts of access, in ways to handle growth in information. They have revised the means by which they accomplish the traditional functions of librarianship, such as cataloging, acquisitions, and reference. One of the most pervasive changes that has accompanied technological development has been in the realm of personnel management. Most, if not all, of the functions of libraries have been affected by technology and have necessitated staff education and training, alterations in job descriptions, and revisions in work flow. Because of the nature of the above changes, many libraries have added specialists to their staffs to manage automation projects.

The articles in this issue address many of the facets of administering automation activities in libraries. This paper focuses on one aspect of the automation librarian's appointment—salary. Recently a couple of papers have appeared which address the issue of librarian salaries in general[1] and salaries for public librarians.[2] Since the position of automation librarian is a specialized one, specific, specialized requirements can become a part of the job announcement. The more stringent the requirements, the smaller the potential market. This is true not only for automation librarians (and librarians generally), but for virtually all jobs. If a library is searching for

John M. Budd is Assistant Professor in the University of Arizona Graduate Library School, Tucson, AZ.

21

someone to fill the position of head of the reference department, for instance, the pool of potential applicants is effectively limited to those with interest in the reference function. If three years prior experience is also required, the pool is further narrowed. If supervisory experience is an additional requirement, the pool becomes smaller still. Geographical considerations will also affect the number of potential applicants. Salary is bound to be a determining factor affecting applicant pools as well.

This paper examines advertisements for automation librarians (also frequently titled systems librarians) in three publications which regularly include advertisements for library positions: *American Libraries*, *Library Hotline*, and *College & Research Libraries News*. Examination of these three titles for the calendar year 1988 yields eighty-four position advertisements. Fifty-three of the ads are from academic libraries, twenty-five are from public libraries (including state library agencies), and six are from special libraries. These eighty-four positions may not comprise all automation librarian openings in 1988, but it is assumed that these are likely to be representative of all positions open. There are some vagaries inherent in advertisements that must be acknowledged. Most ads include a minimum salary; others include a salary range. The figure analyzed here for each advertisement is the minimum. It may well be that the successful applicant is offered an amount of money exceeding the minimum.

These caveats stated, the eighty-four position advertisements can be analyzed. The mean for this body of positions is $27,568 (with a median of $26,000 and a standard deviation of $6,970). This is above the 1987 mean of $22,440 for graduates of accredited library education programs.[3] It also exceeds the mean salary for beginning librarians of $20,346 reported in the 1988 *ALA Survey of Librarian Salaries*.[4] That the salary for automation librarians is greater than those for beginning professionals and for new graduates is not surprising, since the automation position is a specialized one.

How does this salary compare to others in libraries, though? A reasonable comparison might be made between the mean exhibited in the advertisements and that for the heads of library departments. The 1988 *ALA Survey* presents data on more than three thousand branch heads (including heads of departmental libraries) and department heads (a category that includes the library's "Systems office"). The mean salary for this group is $29,318.[5] It should be reiterated that the mean of advertised positions is a result of observing minimum salaries rather than actual job offers. It should also be noted that the ads represent individuals new to library organizations, while the ALA figure includes people who have been in their positions for some time. Lastly, the ads are not exclusively for department head positions; some are for higher and some are for lower ranking positions.

Since this last phenomenon manifests itself, the discrepancy between those positions that are advertised as management positions and those that are less clearly designated can be analyzed. Twenty-nine of the ads state that the position is a head, an assistant or associate director, a manager, or a supervisor. The mean of those ads is $32,425. The mean for the other fifty-three (some of which may be for department heads, but titles such as "Systems Librarian" cannot easily be classified) is $25,007. The following form of the two-sample t test can be used to examine the difference between the two means:

$$SD = \frac{\Sigma x_1^2 + \Sigma x_2^2}{(N_1 - 1) + (N_2 - 1),}$$

$$SE_D = SD \quad \frac{N_1 + N_2}{N_1 \times N_2},$$

$$t = \frac{(M_1 - M_2)}{SE_D},$$

where: SD is the variance (combined standard deviation),
x_1 and x_2 are the differences between each case and the mean for each sample,
N_1 and N_2 are numbers of cases in the samples,
SE_D is the standard error of the difference of the means, and
M_1 and M_2 are the means of the samples.

Employment of this test reveals a t value of 41.450, which indicates a difference that is significant at the .01 level.

As is noted above, different types of libraries are represented in the advertisements. Differences among the types of libraries could be expected and are reflected in the means. The mean salary for the six special library positions is $29,708. The twenty-five public library positions have a mean salary of $26,527. The mean for the fifty-three academic positions is $27,817. While the special library ads may be too few in number to be representative, the t test can be used to examine the difference between means of public and academic library jobs. The resulting t value is 0.746, which does not indicate a significant difference (at the .05 level).

The academic library mean can be compared to some existing academic library salary data. According to the *Annual Salary Survey, 1987* of the Association of Research Libraries (ARL), the projected average salary for fifty-two "Computer" department heads for the 1988 fiscal year is $43,163.[6] Automation positions may also fall into the categories "Other" department head (the mean salary for which is $34,320) and "Functional Specialist" (which has an average salary of $31,396). They may also be filled at the Associate or Assistant Director level. Assuming that the "Computer" department head category is the most descriptive and that most of the automation positions in ARL institutions fall into this category, the average salary is an attractive one. In fact, among all positions noted, it ranks below only Director, Associate Director, and Assistant Director.

Salaries for automation librarian position in academic libraries can also be compared with some other academic librarian salaries. A report of a College and University Personnel Association survey includes median salaries for five library positions: circulation ($24,205), acquisitions ($27,000), technical services ($27,774), public services ($30,000), and reference ($25,803).[7] The median salary for the fifty-three academic library advertisements is $26,000. As with other comparisons, it must be noted that the medians for the five positions reflect salaries of experienced librarians; the advertised openings reflect minimum starting salaries.

In examining automation librarian positions it is necessary to go beyond salaries. Advertisements include requirements of successful candidates; these can be analyzed, as can the monetary rewards apparent from the ads. There are four requirements that are mentioned in ads more frequently than any other: possession of an MLS degree (mentioned sixty-six times), experience with or knowledge of library automation (fifty-two), previous library experience (thirty-five), and ability to communicate well (twenty-eight). These most frequently mentioned requirements center primarily on organizational (library) criteria. While not all of the eighty-four notices require the library degree that is de rigueur for other library positions—in fact, some advertisements stipulate that other master's degrees, notably in computer science, can be substituted for the MLS—education based on library and information science is deemed appropriate in 78.6% of the ads. The requirement of communication ability may be important, but it is one that is implicit in any position in any profession.

In addition to the four requirements noted above, job advertisements include seventeen other requirements, though none of these is mentioned with great frequency. Table 1 includes these seventeen, along with the number of times each is mentioned. The diversity of needs, or at least the diversity of perceived needs, of libraries is reflected in the table. Some ads include rather nebulous requirements, such as negotiation skills, while others are very definite in what they want, such as applicants with driver's licenses. In some instances, the requirements indicate the place of the automation position within the organization. For instance, there is a different organizational slant between one library requiring circulation experience and one requiring technical services experience. It should be noted that this list is comprised only of *requirements*, not desired or preferred knowledge and skill.

All of the above can illustrate something of the nature of the automation position: salaries vary among types of libraries, salaries vary depending on the place of the position within the library, and requirements may vary depending on the needs of individual libraries. There remains a problem with the information available thus far—it is at best relative only to some other library positions. As is evident from the requirements, libraries are somewhat flexible in the hiring of an automation librarian. The successful applicant may not have an MLS degree; so, the desired pool of applicants

Table 1

Additional Advertised Position Requirements

Requirement	Number
Administrative Ability/ Supervisory Experience	12
Programming Experience	11
Technical Service Knowledge/Experience	9
Familiarity with OCLC	6
Knowledge of MARC	6
Driver's License	3
Circulation Knowledge/Experience	2
Master's Degree in Computer Science	2
State Library Certification	2
Ability to Teach Automation Skills	1
Analytical Ability	1
Experience with NOTIS	1
Experience with Staff Training	1
Knowledge of Online Systems	1
Negotiation Skills	1

could include individuals educated in different disciplines. If this is the case, libraries are, in effect, in competition with other fields for people with certain knowledge and/or experience. Assuming that there is some degree of competition, how well are libraries likely to fare when up against other types of employers?

Whereas the average salary for automation librarians reflected in position advertisements is $27,568, the average starting salary for new MBAs in 1987 was $30,400.[8] In March of 1989 this average had climbed to $33,068 for MBAs with little or no experience and with non-technical undergraduate majors.[9] The average for inexperienced MBAs with technical undergraduate majors was $37,993 in March 1989.[10] Individuals with other educational preparation may provide a clearer picture of the competitive factor that must be recognized in recruiting qualified automation librarians. In March 1989 the average job offer to recipients of master's degrees in computer science was $35,105.[11] This is substantially more than the figure computed from the job ads for library positions. Also, previous experience is a requirement for many of the library jobs, whereas it may not be for positions outside libraries.

The above comparison is offered as information that may be illustrative of potential applicant pools. If library administrators wish to open the search to include applicants with educational background different from, or in addition to, library education, then potential applicants are likely to do some comparison shopping with regard to salaries. Certainly money is not the sole motivating force leading individuals into the career paths they choose, but, just as certainly, it is among the variables weighed in making job choices. This presents a dilemma for many library managers. The position of automation librarian is a specialized one, one that often requires knowledge and experience that is different from that of other library professionals. In order to compete for the relatively few such individuals on the market, it is reasonable to look to higher starting salaries. This action carries with it some dangers, though. It may be difficult for library managers to coax funding agencies to free the necessary sums of money in order to attract the kind of applicants who would have a good chance of succeeding in the position. Even when such funding is available, there is the potential for staff unrest when it becomes known that the library is advertising a salary for a new position that may be substantially higher than the existing salaries of some experienced individuals on hand. There is anecdotal evidence to suggest that, at least in some instances, advertised salaries are lower than they might otherwise be because of the existing salary structure within the library.

An easy solution to this problem would be if the salaries of all library personnel could be elevated. This, however, is not likely to occur. Nancy Van House has observed that the library labor market is segmented. One outcome of this is that, "Segmentation affects salary determination by preventing people from moving from lower to higher salary segments.''[12] One of the manifestations of the segmentation is the differences among types of libraries—salaries are not equal, or necessarily equivalent, in academic, public, and special libraries. It may well be, though, that a library manager in a large academic library and one in a medium-sized public will seek individuals with very similar qualities for automation positions. The very natures of the libraries may serve to skew the competition for those individuals. The presence of such a specialization as automation librarianship may further segment the labor market by creating a separate sector which, in some respects, transcends type-of-library segmentation. There are implications here for future investigation. As Van House states, "Research into librarian salary differences must address the issue of how librarians come to choose or to be assigned to sectors.''[13]

This may be a particularly problematic area of research since the position of automation librarian is sufficiently new that a number of the potential applicants are making adjustments in the course of their professional careers; not all of the applicant pool consists of individuals who made an initial decision while still in the educational process. Also problematic is the realization that some degree of automation or technological competence, if not expertise, is becoming pervasive throughout the library organization. This is evident in some of the other papers in this issue. Eventually this may serve to break down some of the existing segmentation, but the near future does not promise a smoothing of the library labor market. The data presented here, then, can be instructive to library managers in determining certain salary thresholds, since these data are meant to be reflective of current hiring practices. It is important, though, to go beyond a cursory glance at the data and to look at the factor of competition and of market segmentation. The position of automation librarian has become one that libraries cannot do without; it no longer suffices to discuss coming technology when automated systems can be seen as virtual mainstays of libraries. The issue for the future, as evidenced by this collection of papers, is how to make organizational decisions with technology in mind. This is true of salaries for new and existing personnel as well.

NOTES

1. John M. Budd, "The Best and the Brightest," *Library Administration and Management* 2 (March 1988): 103-04.

2. John M. Budd, "The Reward Is in the Doing: Public Libraries and Salaries," *Public Libraries* 28 (January/February 1989): 34-38.

3. Carol L. Learmont and Stephen Van Houten, "Placements and Salaries 1987: The Upswing Continues," *Library Journal* 113 (October 15, 1988): 29.

4. American Library Association, Office for Research and Office for Library Personnel Resources, *ALA Survey of Librarian Salaries 1988* (Chicago: ALA, 1988), p. 26.

5. *ALA Survey*, p. 12.

6. Association of Research Libraries, *ARL Annual Salary Survey 1987* (Washington, DC: ARL, 1988), p. 28.

7. Mary Jo Lynch, "Academic Librarian Salaries, 1987-1988," *College & Research Libraries News* 50 (February 1989): 123.

8. Bernie J. Grablowsky, "The Market for MBAs: The Myths and Realities," *Journal of Financial Education* 17 (Fall 1988): 60.

9. College Placement Council, Inc., *CPC Salary Survey* (March 1989): 34.

10. *CPC Salary Survey*, p. 34.

11. *CPC Salary Survey*, p. 35.

12. Nancy Van House, "Labor Market Segmentation and Librarian Salaries," *Library Quarterly* 57 (April 1987): 186.

13. Van House, p. 187.

Personnel and Technology:
An Opportunity for Innovation

Jennifer Cargill

INTRODUCTION

Predicting the future in a society experiencing an accelerating rate of change is risky and fraught with danger in the best of circumstances. Change will affect libraries more dramatically than can be fully envisioned from the perspective of the last decade of the twentieth century. Librarians can hypothesize about the future of libraries and the profession but cannot accurately speculate or fully comprehend the range of challenges and opportunities ahead. However, today's library staff can anticipate that the rest of their careers will be spent in libraries that are undergoing dramatic change, change dictated by technology, by new approaches to research, by demands for information, by different means of accessing that information, by availability of resources.

The increased reliance on automation to access databases of library collections and the use of technology to access other information sources in a variety of formats—including some now unknown—will impact service patterns, create new organizational issues, and affect staffing expectations. Indeed the evolving role of libraries and librarianship in the Information Age should be motivators for service innovations as library administrators analyze the needs of present and future library constituencies. These changing roles will require a commitment that in turn will demand personal and professional growth on the part of staff and a willingness to adapt to the future expectations of libraries and librarians. Library

Jennifer Cargill is Associate University Librarian, Rice University, Houston, TX.

31

staff's own philosophies and approaches will also be affected by many external forces within the environment.

ENVIRONMENT

Transition and change have already become a way of life, the normal flow of work and life, a routine to which individuals must become accustomed if they haven't already. Lives revolve around mobility, transition and change; the lives of many people today may seem unstable, tumultuous. For many people the very thought of remaining in a position or a life that is geared to maintaining the status quo is frightening.

However, even today in the environment of change and transition, the lives of some people may continue to follow a fairly predictable and stable path while the lives of others may have taken turbulent twists and turns. Still others may reach a point in life where they experience a life or career crisis, a crisis that may be primarily focused in the work place or in personal life, or may impinge on both.

Similarly, some libraries may have continued a fairly placid existence, only marginally affected by technology and new approaches to information needs. Automation may have bypassed them; research and curriculum approaches may still be structured traditionally or financial constraints may have hindered automation plans. Other libraries have seized upon the introduction of automation to restructure, to devise new approaches to service, and may be contemplating additional innovations.

These transitions and changes should be viewed as an assist in focusing work lives, helping bring issues into perspective. The transitions and changes in libraries should be viewed as opportunities to become dynamic partners in information delivery. Stability is — and will remain — an illusion. Library staffs, and the libraries in which they work, will be in a period of transition in their libraries and careers. Anticipating being prepared, and understanding the process will assist them in adapting to the transition and change process.

Three major areas are of primary concern in focusing on personnel and technology and the opportunities presented for innovation. All are affected and influenced by present and future constituencies:

- Service options/innovations
- Organizational opportunities
- Staffing concerns

All are affected by—as well as being influential toward—future constituencies.

SERVICE INNOVATIONS

Libraries have been regarded as repositories of information, paper-oriented as represented by books, and periodicals, with some media. These repositories have often been regarded as warehouses; library staff labored to build large collections, both broad and deep, to serve the needs of patrons. Elaborate analysis and statistical programs have been developed to validate the expertise of library staffs in acquiring and servicing these collections.

Libraries have utilized automation to organize and access these vast storage warehouses and to meet immediate information citation needs by delving into subject databases. An increasingly sophisticated clientele can access these databases without relying upon the library staff for assistance. Libraries that were paper-dependent, secure havens of stability have evolved toward a dependence upon technology. The work lives of library staff and their livelihood revolve around miniaturization, computerization and telecommunications.

To justify the continued existence of these collections and the accompanying staff that have been accumulated, administrators must analyze present service patterns, considering how these have evolved, based on the history and mission of the library and institution of which the library is a part.

- What services are currently offered?

  on location
  off site

- Have the interests of the library's constituency changed in recent years?
- Do operational hours—both building and database access

hours — meet the needs of clientele in supplying information to patrons?
• Are the available resources increasing or declining — or increasing at such a minimal rate that they are in effect declining?

In the public areas of libraries, meeting the needs of clientele will remain a priority but the approaches libraries take to provide service must be different. These approaches to servicing patrons' needs will of necessity change since clientele will have dramatically different and escalating expectations. Libraries will be regarded as a link, a module within the total information network upon which each individual will become increasingly reliant. Service plan options must be developed to help direct staff energies.

What might be some of these service options?

1. Electronic Mail

As staff provide reference on a walk up or phone in basis, reference service points are often teeming with patrons awaiting service, phones buzzing with queries. Through the use of electronic mail, patrons will routinely deposit queries for information, and await response from the library's service points. The actual points of service patrons can access will potentially become infinite since they can direct queries to the best possible source of information such as to specialized collections or even to service points that have been established solely to respond to electronic queries.

As more complex, detailed information is required, patrons will have the option of accessing specialized information centers and libraries worldwide. In turn changes in funding for these centers must be explored, perhaps fee-based upon access by patrons, or more tax-supported funding with codes or passwords replacing the traditional library card. National and international online libraries or information centers will be created. Without a readily identifiable local constituency, funding for these information centers will become an issue during the Information Age. The eventual outcome may be an approach similar to that currently accepted for cable television or "payment per episode" viewing, with availability scrambled to all but those with the access code. Libraries created for and limited to specific clientele groups will either revise their policies or devise access blocks or codes, preventing or limiting electronic queries.

Queries for information and the resulting responses will be input and received twenty-four hours a day, seven days a week. Individuals will become consumers of information and will expect—with the zeal of the activist consumer—to be satisfied. As the expectation or satisfaction levels rise, expediting information from storage point to consumer will become a priority.

Reference aids will be available online for library user and bibliographic instruction and basic reference queries. General directional assistance including floor plans will be online from remote locations as well as onsite.

2. Support for Electronic Studios and Workstations

The lifestyles of a library's clients will affect our services. Patrons might be a few buildings away—or hundreds of miles distant. They may work in an office or other organizational environment or may work from the comfort of their home or while in transit.

As clientele work in electronic studios at scholars' workstations, becoming accustomed to almost instantaneous access to the information that is needed, library staffs will experience the rising expectation level impacting on the services offered. The use of technology will make instantaneous provision of information possible: through electronic query or consultation, database access, document delivery, etc.

As patrons become accustomed to almost instantaneous access to information, followed by provision of full text, they will also come to rely upon laptops for note taking and composition. These portable workstations will be available for patrons to check out and use during onsite use of collections.

Online learning packages will provide directional or instructional guidance in utilizing technological developments.

3. Database Access

Patrons will directly access databases and download data needed to resolve problems or support individual lifestyles. Additional databases will be created with much of their formulation being done automatically with programs similar to indexing programs. Libraries will participate in the creation process by serving as test sites for developing or testing new databases, responding to patron needs.

4. SDI

The demands of clients will necessitate routinely offered selective dissemination of information [SDI] services, client-specific and machine-generated. Interest profiles will be established for constituents; these SDI services will become particularly critical with some types of information, such as government documents and the increasingly important gray literature. Furthermore, provision of these SDI services will become integral parts of grant proposals, and for support of awarded grants. Libraries will participate in the refinement of SDI services by being test sites for prototypes of SDI systems.

5. Document/Information Delivery

Those SDI services as well as the utilization of workstations by our patrons will lead to sophisticated document delivery systems since clients will not be content to have the citations available on-line. Libraries will develop their own delivery systems as well as working with document providers. Document delivery will evolve from

- the traditional provision of books and copies, delivered by staff within a geographic area,
- to high speed facsimile delivery as telefacsimile equipment becomes as prevalent as the telephone,
- to full text available through scanning into machine-readable form or through access to gigantic full text files, an expansion of present full text capabilities.

Libraries will become partners with other libraries in establishing remote storage facilities supported by document delivery systems that must become more efficient to service these warehouses of materials.

Librarians will have the ability to analyze the collections broadly and in depth. They will have the options through automation to create quick citation lists and selection guides, identifying last copies for preservation purposes, and comparing collections for resource sharing. This will enable collection development librarians to have more time for selecting retrospectively or within narrow specialities, preparing budget projections, and justifying major expenditures for collections or for loading new databases.

Support of the Information Process

There is potential for the library to become the supportive foundation for the searching and information access process for a large portion of society. This will revitalize use of library collections, but won't it also potentially create two segments within society, two segments separated by a channel of information darkness? Society will run the risk of becoming *inclusive* in the provision of information, since potentially everyone will have the opportunity to gain access to information available in many formats, through different delivery modes, and libraries might find that they are inundated with clients. There will also be created an *exclusive* segment of society, where the educated and technologically literate, those who are aggressive, affluent, and privileged enough will have access and the ability to utilize information on demand.

Will there then be the risk of technological intervention, either blatant or by default, that will create a new type of censorship or information control? Will a danger exist of disenfranchising segments of society by de facto limiting the availability of information to patrons? What will be the effect upon library resource sharing agreements and interlibrary loan if clients can access information themselves and request document delivery from many service points?

There will evolve a recognition that information is not free in the Information Age as service options and information demands are reviewed. The end result will potentially be creation of a hierarchy of information needs, with accompanying cost levels specified.

Interaction Modes

While library reference or information centers become an oasis populated with clusters of workstations for on site use, staff will expand its role in end user training. In libraries supporting the education process, library staff will closely interact with instructors in the curriculum planning process to direct end user efforts, helping through managing information access.

At the same time, as libraries move from traditional reference service, they will increasingly provide an appointment level consultation service for papers and projects—where the librarian works directly with clients on a one-to-one basis to identify and define the information needs of the individual, formulate an access methodology, and direct the client to the appropriate resources, utilizing document delivery.

The use of the team approach in the education process will become increasingly prevalent. In either approach—the librarian assisting users at a workstation cluster or the librarian consulting with a client at a workstation, in an office, or via electronic mail—the librarian will become an integral part of the education process as the team member who is responsible for managing information access.

The service innovations incorporated into libraries in the future and the new demands placed on library staff will bring about a "creative tension" which can—and probably will—lead to high stress levels among staff and constituents. Staff will sometimes find themselves scrambling to familiarize themselves with a system before client demands exceed staff abilities to assist with information delivery. It will become essential for libraries to capitalize upon this "creative tension" to devise additional service innovations.

Thus, service innovations for future constituencies will progress from:

- the current status,
- to the introduction of service innovations,
- to the availability of a menu of service options,
- to institutionalization of these innovations/options, and
- to — finally — advocacy for additional innovations.

It is critical for libraries to foster a creative atmosphere so more service innovations will be explored and devised.

ORGANIZATIONAL OPPORTUNITIES

Service innovations will in turn lead to organizational issues, among which will be these:

- Diversity of services offered
- Marketing the services
- An entrepreneurial spirit
- Organizational structure
- Funding alternatives

If libraries are to compete successfully against other information brokers, the services offered must be diverse but manageable within the resources available to the library. The services must be marketed so potential clients are aware not only what is available but how they can benefit from the services offered. Marketing is an area where librarians presently have marginal expertise; additional skills must be developed.

Once again "creative tension" can be utilized as the services to be offered are identified, services that will anticipate and meet the needs of clients. Libraries and library staff will become entrepreneurial, anticipating and creating services not yet offered, but services for which a demand can be created.

The organization itself can capitalize upon this "creative tension" to create an atmospheric climate in which innovation is expected and is rewarded. Innovation through new ideas must be immediately followed by planning how the services will be implemented and then how the resulting demand levels will be met.

The organization will of necessity have to redefine its role and the role of staff. Reorganization of the institutional structure will evolve from the process of creating and implementing new service options. Different authority lines, blurring of some lines, merging of units, sharing of responsibilities are among some of the changes that may take place.

Alternative funding may be required—which may be still another place that an entrepreneurial approach can be considered—by creating services that can contribute income as a result of demands for the new services.

STAFFING CONCERNS

Organizational issues in turn result in staffing concerns. Staff reacting to service innovations and reactions to organizational restructuring will lead to questions concerning personal adjustments. If staff understand the coping process, they will adjust more easily. Staff will undergo several steps in the coping process:

1. The first will be a period of losing focus, maintaining the status quo as they try to continue life as usual, ignoring or denying the changes around them. In this period staff may experience doubt about the direction service innovations are evolving.

2. From that stage, most staff will move to a point of willingness to put the past behind them and move forward.

3. That will be followed by a period of momentum when staff enjoy the new experiences and build confidence in innovations in information provision. They learn to compensate for disappointments and frustrations and still maintain forward momentum.

4. After a period of success, they will reach the point of stepping aside—outside the situation—to analyze the experience, learning from the positive and negative aspects.

5. Then staff will reach a period where the experience has been institutionalized.

6. Finally staff will enter a period of advocacy where they eagerly share the experience with others and help direct others through similar evolutions.

Knowing how the library and the profession are changing, having an awareness of their own personal adjustment mechanism, and understanding the coping process will make the transition through change easier. This coping process is similar to the process of instilling innovations into the organization.

FUTURE NEEDS

In the libraries that will be serving future constituencies, there will be more emphasis on focused service for the user rather than reactive service to the organization. To have available staff concerned with this style of service provision, an educational process that will retrain existing staff and create appropriate education and training for potential staff to meet library needs must be established. Staff skilled intellectually with subject expertise or technological prowess will be needed. Those who have highly developed interaction skills, are proactive toward their constituencies, and are naturally flexible and responsive in their approach to diverse service requirements will be in demand. As practitioners, today's librarians should encourage graduate schools to offer courses emphasizing nontraditional services, teaching skills that will prepare the graduates for a variety of service offerings and for assignments in bridge positions where they will work in more than one functional area.

Even if libraries provide service options, cope with organizational reaction and needs, and hire additional staff with the necessary skills, administrators must still manage to retain staff for a reasonable length of time. Thus, retention becomes an issue. Once the staff to provide service innovations and cope with organizational change are on hand, administrators will face the need to stimulate them to new growth, keep them interested and challenged, always in quest of alternatives to serving our constituencies — and fostering an entrepreneurial attitude. To provide a pool of talent, libraries must recruit actively to attract additional people to the profession, hire people committed to the new service options, and assist them in maintaining an enthusiastic commitment to the concept of service innovations in an Information Age.

The next decade will lead to dramatic changes in the structure of library organizations and service techniques. The end result will be a few libraries that adhere to traditionalism and fear risk taking, becoming backwater libraries, isolated from the mainstream rather than capitalizing on the opportunities of the Information Age. Other libraries that are committed to meeting the expectations of their clientele will become leaders/initiators/innovators in the Information World.

Four points must be kept in mind as libraries approach the future:

1. The expanding environment will place new and different demands and constraints on libraries.

2. The missions and goals of libraries will broaden considerably.

3. New technologies will impose new data and behavior requirements — and will make possible new demands.

4. People with diverse educational backgrounds, expectations, and attitudes will become potential clients — and members of library staffs.

In turn, library administrators must determine whether we:

• are pursuing worthwhile goals;
• are aware of the short- and long-term organizational effects;
• can recognize the snowball effect that will result from the offered service options;
• will maintain the creative tension . . . and . . . ;
• have the resources available to cope with innovation.

[AUTHOR'S NOTE: Familiarity with the change process and the impact technology has on people is essential in managing personnel in highly technical libraries. The suggested background sources will assist the administrator in gaining insight into the process.]

SUGGESTED SOURCES

Adams, John A. and Spencer, Sabina A. "People in Transition." *Training & Development.* 42 (October 1988): 61-63.

Atkinson, Hugh C. "The Impact of New Technology on Library Organization." *The Bowker Annual of Library & Book Trade Information.* 29th ed. New York: Bowker, 1984, pp. 109-114.

Baird, Lloyd and Kram, Kathy. "Career Dynamics: Managing the Superior/Subordinate Relationship." *Organizational Dynamics.* 11 (Spring 1983): 46-64.

Berg, Per-Olof. "Symbolic Management of Human Resources," *Human Resource Management.* 25 (Winter 1986):557-79.

Bichtler, Julie. "Technostress in Libraries: Causes, Effects, and Solutions." *The Electronic Library.* 5 (October 1987): 282-287.

Bradford, David L. and Cohen, Allen R. *Managing for Excellence: The Guide to*

Developing High Performance in Contemporary Organizations. New York: John Wiley, 1984.

Brianas, James. "Mastering 'Dynamic Complexity;' the Key to Managing Change." *International Management.* 41 (October 1986): 88.

Bridges, William. "Managing Organizational Transitions." *Organizational Dynamics.* 15 (Summer 1986): 24-33.

Burke, W. Warner. *Organization Development: A Normative View.* Reading, Ma: Addison-Wesley Publishing Company, 1987.

Busch, Joe. "Coming Out of the Back Room: Management Issues for Technical Services in the Eighties." *Technical Services Quarterly.* 2 (Spring-Summer 1985): 115-41.

Cargill, Jennifer. "Developing Library Leaders: The Role of Mentorship." *Library Administration and Management.* 3 (Winter 1989): 12-15.

———. "Use of a Proactive Analysis Process in Human Resources Management." *Technical Services Quarterly.* 5 (Summer 1988): 3-13.

——— and Webb, Gisela. *Managing Libraries in Transition.* Phoenix, AZ: Oryx Press, 1988.

Cherrington, David S. *Work Ethics: Working Values and Values that Work.* New York: AMACOM, 1980.

Conroy, Barbara. "The Human Element: Staff Development in the Electronic Library." *Drexel Library Quarterly.* 17 (Fall 1981): 91-106.

Cornish, Edward. "The Library of the Future." *The Futurist.* 19 (December 1985): 2.

Darling, John R., and Cluff, E. Dale. "Managing Interpersonal Conflict in a University Library." *Library Administration and Management.* 1 (January 1987): 16-22.

Davis, Peter. "Libraries at the Turning Point: Issues in Proactive Planning." *Journal of Library Administration.* 1 (Summer 1980): 11-24.

Drucker, Peter F. "The Coming of the New Organization." *Harvard Business Review.* 66 (January-February 1988): 45-53.

Dwyer, James R. "The Evolutionary Role of Technical Services." *Journal of Library Administration.* 9 (1988): 13-26.

Fayen, Emily Gallup. "Beyond Technology: Rethinking 'Librarian'." *American Libraries.* 17 (April 1986): 240-2.

Featherston, H. Joe, and Bednarek, Robert J. "A Positive Demonstration of Concern for Employees." *Personnel Administrator.* 26 (September 1981): 43-47.

Fine, Sara F. "Technological Innovation, Diffusion, and Resistance: An Historical Perspective." *Journal of Library Administration.* 7 (Spring 1986): 83-108.

Fisher, K. Kim. "Management Roles in the Implementation of Participative Management Systems." *Human Resource Management.* 25 (Fall 1986): 459-79.

Foster, Richard N. *Innovation: the Attacker's Advantage.* New York: Summit Books, 1986.

Freedman, Maurice J. "Automation and the Future of Technical Services." *Library Journal.* 109 (June 15, 1984): 1197-1203.

Gibson, Jane Whitney, and Hodgetts, Richard M. *Organizational Communications: A Managerial Perspective*. Orlando, Fl: Academic Press, 1986.

Goldsmith, Vern. *Effective Team Building*. New York: American Management Associations Extension Institute, 1980.

Gorman, Michael. "The Ecumenical Librarian." *Reference Librarian*. 9 (Fall/Winter 1983): 55-64.

———, ed. *Library Technical Services in the Late 1980s: Toward the 21st Century*. Englewood, CO: Libraries Unlimited, 1989.

———. "On Doing Away with Technical Services Departments." *American Libraries*. 10 (July/August 1979): 435-437.

Hacken, Richard D. "Tomorrow's Research Library: Vigor or Rigor Mortis?" *College and Research Libraries*. 49 (November 1988): 485-493.

Hendrick, Clyde. "The Library in the Twenty-First Century." *College and Research Libraries*. 47 (March 1986): 127-131.

Hersey, Paul, and Blanchard, Kenneth H. *Management of Organizational Behavior: Utilizing Human Resources*. 3d ed. Englewood Cliffs, NJ: Prentice-Hall, 1977.

Horny, Karen L. "Managing Change: Technology and the Profession." *Library Journal*. 110 (October 1, 1985): 56-58.

Hornstein, Harvey A. *Managerial Courage*. New York: John Wiley & Sons, 1986.

Hunt, James Gerald, et al., eds. *Emerging Leadership Vistas*. Lexington, MA: Lexington Books, 1988.

Hyatt, James A., and Santiago, Aurora A. *University Libraries in Transition*. Washington, DC: National Association of College and University Business Officers, 1987.

Kanter, Rosabeth Moss. *The Change Masters: Innovation and Entrepreneurship in the American Corporation*. New York: Simon and Schuster, 1983.

———. "The New Workforce Meets the Changing Workplace: Strains, Dilemmas, and Contradictions in Attempts to Implement Participative and Entrepreneurial Management." *Human Resources Management*. 25 (Winter 1986): 515-37.

Kets de Vries, Manfred et al. "Using the Life Cycle to Anticipate Satisfaction at Work." *Journal of Forecasting*. 3 (1984): 161-72.

Likert, Rensis. *The Human Organization: Its Management and Value*. New York: McGraw-Hill, 1967.

Losoncy, Lewis. *The Motivating Leader*. Englewood Cliffs, NJ: Prentice-Hall, 1985.

Lowry, Charles B. "Technology in Libraries: Six Rules for Management." *Library Hi Tech*. 3 (1985): 27-29.

McCombs, Gillian. "Public and Technical Services: Disappearing Barriers." *Wilson Library Bulletin*. 61 (November 1986): 25-28.

Maccoby, Michael. "Leadership Needs of the 1980s." *Current Issues in Higher Education* 1 (1979): 17-23.

Malinconico, S. Michael. "People and Machines: Changing Relationships." *Library Journal*. 108 (December 1, 1983): 2222-2224.

Martell, Charles. "Investing in People." *Journal of Academic Librarianship*. 9 (March 1983): 33-35.

Matejko, Alexander. *The Self-Defeating Organization*. New York: Praeger, 1986.

Migneault, Robert LaLiberte. "Humanistic Management by Teamwork in Academic Libraries." *Library Administration and Management*. 2 (June 1988): 132-136.

Morf, Martin. *Optimizing Work Performance: A Look Beyond the Bottom Line*. New York: Quorum Books, 1986.

Nanus, Burt. "Doing the Right Thing." *The Bureaucrat*. 15: (Fall 1986): 9-12.

Olsgaard, John N. "Automation as a Socio-Organizational Agent of Change: An Evaluative Literature Review." *Information Technology and Libraries*. 4 (March 1985): 19-28.

Pascarella, Perry. *The New Achievers: Creating a Modern Work Ethic*. New York: Free Press, 1984.

Portnoy, Robert A. *Leadership: What Every Leader Should Know about People*. Englewood Cliffs, NJ: Prentice-Hall, 1986.

Quick, Thomas L. *Inspiring People at Work: How to Make Participative Management Work for You*. New York: Executive Enterprises Publications, 1986.

_____. *Managing People at Work Desk Guide*. New York: Executive Enterprises Publications, 1983.

Rasberry, Robert W., and Lemoine, Laura Fletcher. *Effective Managerial Communication*. Boston: Kent Publishing, 1986.

Riggs, Donald E. *Library Leadership: Visualizing the Future*. Phoenix, AZ: Oryx Press, 1982.

_____. *Strategic Planning for Library Managers*. Phoenix, AZ: Oryx Press, 1984.

Rooks, Dana C. and Thompson, Linda L. "Impact of Automation on Technical Services." *Journal of Library Administration*. 9 (1988): 121-136.

Segal, JoAnn and Tyson, John. "The Library's Changing Role in Higher Education." *Library Journal*. 110 (September 15, 1985): 44-46.

Shaughnessy, Thomas W. "Technology and the Structure of Libraries." *Libri*. 32 (1982): 149-155.

Schneier, Craig Eric; Beatty, Richard W.; and McEnvoy, Glenn M. *Personnel/Human Resources Management Today: Readings and Commentary*. 2d ed. Reading, MA: Addison-Wesley, 1986.

Shapero, Albert. *Managing Professional People*. New York: Free Press, 1985.

Stewart, Douglas. *The Power of People Skills: A Manager's Guide to Assessing and Developing Your Organization's Greatest Resource*. New York: John Wiley & Sons, 1986.

Townley, Charles T. "Nuturing Library Effectiveness: Leadership for Personnel Development." *Library Administration and Management*. 3 (Winter 1989): 16-20.

Veaner, Allen B. "1985 to 1995: The Next Decade in Academic Librarianship, Part I. 46 (May 1985): 209-229; and Part II. 46 (July 1985): 295-307.

Webb, Gisela. "Educating Librarians and Support Staff for Technical Services." *Journal of Library Administration.* 9 (1988): 111-120.

White, Herbert S. "Defining Basic Competencies." *American Libraries.* 14 (September 1983): 519-525.

————. *Library Personnel Management.* White Plains, NY: Knowledge Industry, 1985.

Williams, James W. "The Decentralization of Selected Technical Services at the University of Illinois at Urbana-Champaign." *Technical Services Quarterly.* 4 (Summer 1987): 5-19.

Wynn, Richard and Guditus, Charles W. *Team Management: Leadership by Consensus.* Columbus, OH: Charles E. Merrill, 1984.

Yankelovich, Daniel. *New Rules, Searching for Self-Fulfilment in a World Turned Upside Down.* New York: Random House, 1981.

Yukl, Gary A. *Leadership in Organizations.* Englewood Cliffs, NJ: Prentice-Hall, 1981.

Zuboff, Shoshana. "New Worlds of Computer-Mediated Work." *Harvard Business Review.* 60 (September-October 1982): 142-52.

Jobs and Changes
in the Technological Age

Ann E. Prentice

As we review the literature about the changing nature of the workplace and innovations that have occurred and are reported, much of it relates to changes that are only indirectly related to technology. A study conducted for the American Management Association by Goodmeasure, Inc., Rosabeth Moss Kanter's consulting firm, provides some general conclusions about the state of work in the 1980s in the U.S. with projection to the 1990s.

According to Kanter, the next decade will find numerous alternatives available to workers in the way they can organize their work. Flextime and permanent part time work will be more prevalent work configurations. The project team, which began on the shop floor, will continue to spread to such areas as government agencies and public utilities. Group problem solving is gaining favor in library-like areas of activity. Work at home is becoming an attractive alternative because of the freedom the computer and facsimile machine afford many individuals.

Innovation in the workplace is more often found in the public sector than the private sector and occurs in either a non-union or a totally unionized environment. Kanter suggests that a mixed union, non-union environment may be a less fertile environment for innovation. The kind of flexibility found in the workplace varies with the size of the organization. While smaller organizations appear to be more willing to consider such activities as work groups or work-at-home activities, the large companies more often offer formal training in such options as participatory management. Those orga-

---

Ann E. Prentice is Associate Vice President for Library and Information Resources at the University of South Florida, Tampa, FL.

© 1990 by The Haworth Press, Inc. All rights reserved.

nizations that can be labeled progressive and are innovators in workplace flexibility tend to be more productive than their more conservative counterparts.[1]

The report of the "Task Force on the New York State Public workplace in the 21st Century"[2] provided by the Professional Development Program of the Rockefeller College of Public Affairs and Policy lists ten guiding principles and fifty-five supporting recommendations for the configuration and management of its public workforce in the next century. Emphasis is placed on recruitment, deployment, education, management style, organizational effectiveness, and compensation. Although technology is not specifically addressed, mention is made that greater flexibility in carrying out assignments be encouraged.

One could look at a large portion of the considerable body of management literature written in the past decade and at the projections into the next century without having any great indication that technology plays a major role in the present and continuing operation of the workplace. This may well be because the planners and managers, the top levels of the workplace, are slow to recognize the impact of technology. They have consistently been found to be the slowest to adopt technological change as it impacts the management of the workplace.

THE CHANGING ENVIRONMENT

Despite these indications, technology is changing the workforce and the workplace. This statement has been true since the beginning of the Industrial Revolution and, in the case of information related activities, has been true since the invention of the printing press more than five hundred years ago. Workers and managers of the workforce have mixed views as to whether technological advances that affect the workplace are positive or negative. Work may be done faster and with greater accuracy, and this is positive. Tasks must be learned and activities realigned, and this is seen by some as a threat. The conventional wisdom of industrialization is that "technological change increases productivity and in doing so requires a broader variety of skills and higher average skills from the workplace.''[3] The application of automation to tasks eliminates much of the routinized work and eliminates many routine jobs. The new jobs that replace routine positions will require a higher level of education. There is a significant lack of individuals entering the workforce who have the required educational skills to fit into this new environment. This is of concern to business and industry and the reason why business leaders are pressuring the education system to upgrade its programs, reduce dropout rates, and graduate individuals who will meet the higher standard of education required in the emerging workplace.

Some see the quality of work downgraded because the human touch, the craft component, is less important. Controlling a chemical process by computer rather than by observing it requires the ability to read into data on a screen those things formerly understood by smelling, seeing, and, in some cases, tasting or touching. The individual is removed from direct interaction with the activity. This may be safer and provide more accurate information, but the satisfaction of direct interaction with the elements of the job is reduced. The worker is no longer a part of the process but is an observer and therefore a less critical player. The worker's response is to say that the product not produced by human hands is of lower quality. The loss of a feeling of human worth is a common and unfortunate byproduct of automation, particularly in the case of routine tasks.

Others see little net change when a technology is introduced into the workplace. Some jobs will change but those changes will be assimilated into the overall activities and there will be little visible difference. This often represents the viewpoint of middle or top management whose views encompass a large portion of the organization or the entire organization rather than being focused on specific tasks.

Regardless of how one views technology, it is an increasingly important aspect of the workplace. To compete with other groups or with other countries, we have no choice but to incorporate technology, computer technology particularly, into all relevant aspects of the workplace. Stress will occur as job change and new learning takes place. Workers may fear job loss or demotion. They may resent having to change their work patterns. Communication patterns among workers may shift. There is no accurate way to gauge the social fallout that will occur with the introduction of technology but it will occur.

The way in which new technology based systems are introduced is critical to the success of the system. There are differing and somewhat antagonistic approaches to technological innovation by those who are technically expert and those who are sensitive to the social and psychological aspects.[4] A too rapid introduction of technology by those who understand technical operations and have convinced managers to adopt a new system before those who will be expected to work with the system are ready for it is a major reason why workers may not be willing to accept the changes that occur. When a new system is discussed by those involved, the need for change is described, appropriate training is made available, and assurances are given about the anticipated outcomes, individuals are more willing to deal with a new technology.

Technology may be adopted by managers because it is assumed to be in the interest of the organization. This may or may not have been discussed by those expected to use it. Even though the innovation may be the latest in "hi-tech" or may have been used successfully in similar environments, the arbitrary or seemingly arbitrary imposition of technology on a group of workers may set up an antagonistic relationship that will limit its success.

Technology has the greatest impact on the lower levels of the occupation chain where work is routine and has less impact at the top where authority and decision making are concentrated.[5] Managers who resist changes that technology may make on their workstyle may be very willing to enforce changes on others. Further, they may not have an adequate understanding of the changes technology makes and may be unsympathetic to the concerns of workers. The majority of the top level managers are older, well educated males[6] — those who are most threatened by changes in the workplace. They are aware of the need to become technologically sophisticated but are often slow to function in the changing environment while at the same time insisting that their staff do so.

THE CHANGING JOB ITSELF

With the addition of computer technology to the workplace, a number of assumptions have been made. There would be a change in job requirements. Some jobs would be phased out and new jobs would emerge. The skill level of jobs would increase and this increase in skill level would result in greater job satisfaction. The workplace would be more efficient and more work of higher quality would be accomplished. These assumptions held by management were more or less acceptable to the managed whose concerns focused on how their particular job would change, what they would need to learn to function in the changing environment, and how closely they would be monitored. The often conflicting objectives and concerns of management, workers, and technologists anxious to impose their particular technology on the workplace has yet to be resolved.

Each new technology has speeded up our ability to produce. Early technology relieved our bodies of tasks of lifting, hauling, and pulling. The automobile and airplane freed us from one work location and the telephone shortened time between communications. Computer technology expands our ability to calculate and to manage processes. It shortens the time needed to organize and complete routine tasks. The speed with which computing can be used to accomplish tasks is increasing exponentially, in the size of the task to be undertaken and the speed with which it can be accomplished. For those who see a wide open future for technology, caution is advised. "Successful managers of the future will increasingly have to be able to manage more information than successful managers of today. Yet, the human capacities of speaking, listening, reading, and writing are likely to remain constant."[7]

THE LIBRARY SETTING

When applying these general findings to the library setting, one quickly finds that there is very little written on managing technology in the library workplace beyond reporting experience and setting guidelines for incorporating a particular technology into the workplace such as an online catalog. There are numerous articles on the impact of automation, but they tend to focus on the changing formats of information rather than on the changing nature of jobs. Libraries are organizations that adopt and adapt rather than serving as sources of innovation. Our planning processes, our budgeting techniques and many of our other management activities are adapted from the for-profit sector. The technology on which our online catalogs are based is derived to a large extent from the business sector, and many of the ways in which we have incorporated other technology are copied as well.

Over the past three decades the library has become more and more dependent on technology. That technology has been used to store information and to develop means of accessing the stored information. Cataloging activities have changed from a manual to an online mode. The balance of professional to non-professional cataloging tasks has changed. With an online catalog there is no longer the need to file cards in the public catalog and then to revise the filing, thus freeing staff from these tasks. Retrospective conversion of materials has produced a number of new tasks. The cataloging department may need fewer original catalogers, fewer filers, and more individuals familiar with OCLC. Within that unit there has usually been considerable change. Within the reference department, there has been the need for the add on skill of on-line searching but other than that, there has been relatively little change in the way we do reference.

We have tried to incorporate technology into the library, a little bit here and a lot there, but have often done so in response to external pressure. We learned DIALOG searching because it was there and we needed to use it. We have gone to online catalogs in large part because of external pressure. What we have not done is to look at the library as a whole and determine if its present configuration is appropriate to the goals and objectives it must meet.

The library's organization has changed little if at all in more than a century. The information explosion has increased the library's size but has not changed its organization. The growth of the universities in size and number has placed an additional burden on libraries to provide service to an ever increasing and increasingly diverse community. These and other major changes have occurred with little or no change in the organization of the library, or for that matter of higher education. What has occurred in the past decade, in addition to adopting online catalogs and becoming expert searchers of bibliographic data bases is that attitudes are changing. We are no longer in awe of technology, although we may not be particularly comfortable with it. We are less fearful that technology will control the workplace than we once were, although we have not yet established our own control over it.

What we must do is look at the library, determine its goals for the next decade, and then review its organization as it relates to that goal. Special attention must be paid to the way in which technology should be incorporated into all activities. Library managers need to understand what a technologically smart workplace is and how to develop the library into such a workplace. Limited expertise is available, and we will need to seek out consultants who can assist in the effort. They tend to be found in business schools and in certain industries such as AT & T whose managers are in the process of defining their own information smart workplace.

As technology is added to the organization, it is often in addition to existing activities as in the case of online searching. New tasks are added to existing job descriptions or new jobs such as online librarian are created. The old tasks and old jobs may or may not go away. The result is an increased workload and a workplace that is on two tracks—the information smart track where one is comfortable with the latest technology and uses it to organize, store, and retrieve information, and the pre-industrial (not just the pre-technical) environment of paper shuffling and card-filing that has been typical of much library activity for centuries.

Within the library, we need to review the workflow, review jobs, and determine how each task contributes to the overall objective. This comprehensive review will reveal overlap in automated and manual activities and will identify gaps that may appear. Levels of staffing may change in the new environment. New job configurations will undoubtedly emerge. New groupings of activity will also emerge as will changed ways of interacting with our publics.

Our publics are also changing in a number of ways. They are more diverse in age, background, and expectations, and they are diverse in their understanding of computer technology. In an academic environment, some faculty are very comfortable with their workstation and use it as an interface with the library through the online catalog. They do their own searching via BRS After Dark, and make their interlibrary loan requests via E-Mail. They communicate with reference and collection development librarians electronically. Working with these faculty in an online environment requires a different type of reference librarian than one who provides service to walk-in faculty and students. As more faculty become comfortable with their workstation and the ways in which they use it to access information, their library connection may well be a subject specialist who is an expert searcher equally at home online and in the stacks. The new "information associates" may be assigned a number of faculty who will be their particular clients. Walk-in service may become less and less common.

Characteristics of future librarians was the topic of a 1984 Association of Research Libraries program. When librarians at Johns Hopkins University reviewed the model developed by ARL, they projected that in the future there would be more expert bibliographers, more highly skilled reference librarians, and librarians who have the technological expertise to design and use linking systems.[8]

With current technology, the branch library may take on an entirely different form. There will be branches throughout the university called "information stations" with a few books and journals for browsing. The "information associate" seated at a terminal will literally have the world of information a keystroke away and will respond to faculty and student needs immediately upon request. Public libraries will have similar "branches" in governmental offices, businesses, and public places such as the Chamber of Commerce. At the same time we will continue to provide service in some of the traditional ways to those who do not have access to a workstation or who wish to have more traditional service.

These examples of new configurations for the 1990s are among a number of possibilities that may emerge as we look at our overall information workplace in the light of technology, of our changing clientele, and in our ability to provide service. As the information base continues to grow, our traditional ways of managing it and its use may no longer suffice and we will need to seek out more appropriate configurations. Numerous new information tools will be available to us, from hypertext to expert systems and beyond. Some will fill our needs while others will not. An overall plan for jobs and technology that results in cost effective, high quality information service is the goal.

The keys to success in this changed environment are planning and training. The need for an overall plan and direction has been discussed. The workplace is a renewable asset, renewable through retraining. A comprehensive action plan for education is essential to insure an appropriate workforce. Learning new skills should benefit the individual in a number of ways: through personal pride and satisfaction, through improved performance, and in an increase in salary. The teaching of new concepts and skills is the responsibility of in-house staff development officers, professional schools, and vendors who will design and implement training programs.

The jobs of tomorrow will, in many ways, be similar to those of today. The environment within which those jobs are performed will have a number of similarities. Libraries have not typically been seen as centers of innovation. Given the nature of the service performed, the current level of technology (albeit not particularly well integrated into the overall library organization), and the experience of librarians in dealing with a diverse group of information seekers, there is an opportunity for the library to be the leader in managing change in information environments and in defining tomorrow's information jobs.

NOTES

1. Goodmeasure, Inc., *The Changing American Workplace: Work Alternatives in the '80's* (New York: American Management Assn., 1985), p. 48.

2. Professional Development Program, Rockefeller College of Public Affairs and Policy, *Summary of Recommendations Produced by the Task Force on the New York State Public Workforce in the 21st Century.* (Albany, N.Y., The College, 1989), p. 1-2.

3. Kenneth I. Spenner, "Deciphering Prometheus: Temporal Change in the Skill Level of Work," *American Sociological Review* 48 (December 1983):824.

4. Frank Blacker and Colin Brown, "Evaluation and Impact of Information Technology on People Organization," *Human Relations* 48 (November 1985):2.

5. William Form and Daniel B. McMullen, "Women, Men, and Machines," *Work and Occupations* 10(1983):149.

6. *Ibid*, p. 170.

7. Richard. C. Huseman and Edward W. Miles, "Organizational Communication in the Information Age; Implications of Computer-Based Systems," *Journal of Management* 14(1988):184.

8. Susan K. Martin, "Library Management and Emerging Technology: The Immovable Force and the Irresistible Object" *Library Trends* 37(Winter 1989):378.

BIBLIOGRAPHY

Blacker, Frank and Colin Brown. "Evaluation and Impact of Information Technology on People in Organizations." *Human Relations* 48 (November 1985):213-231.

Clinic on Library Applications of Data Processing. (Papers Presented at the 22nd Annual Clinic on Library Applications of Data Processing, April 14-16, 1985.) Human Aspects of Library Automation: Helping Staff and Patrons Cope. Edited by Dobora Shaw. Urbana-Champaign, Ill.: University of Illinois Graduate School of Library and Information Science, 1986.

Colton, Joel and Stuart Bruckly eds. *Technology, The Economy and Society; The American Experience*. New York: Columbia University Press, 1987.

Form, William and David B. McMillen. "Women, Men, and Machines." *Work and Occupations* 10, no. 2 (1983):147-178.

Gattiber, Urs E. and Laurel Larewood. *Managing Technological Development: Strategic and Human Resources Issues*. Berlin: Walter de Gruyter, 1988.

Goodmeasure, Inc. *The Changing American Workplace: Work Alternatives in the '80s*. New York: American Management Assn., 1985.

Gutek, Barbara A., Tora K. Bikson, and Don Manben. "Individual and Organizational Consequences of Computer-Based Office Information Technology." *Applied Social Psychology Annual* 5 (1984):231-254.

Huseman, Richard C. and Edward W. Miles. "Organizational Communication in the Information Age: Implications of Computer-Based Systems." *Journal of Management* 14, no 2 (1988):181-204.

Kanter, Rosabeth Moss. *When Giants Learn to Dance; Mastering the Challenge of Strategy, Management and Careers in the 1990's*. New York: Simon and Schuster, 1989.

Markies, M. Lynne and Daniel Robey. "Information Technology and Organizational Change: Causal Structure in Theory and Research." *Management Science* 34, no 5 (May 1989):583-598.

Martin, Susan K. "Library Management and Emerging Technology: the Immovable Force and the Irresistible Object." *Library Trends* 37, no 3 (Winter 1989):374-82.

Monger, Rod F. *Mastering Technology; A Management Framework for Getting Results*. New York: Free Press, 1988.

Olsgaard, John. "Automation as a Socio-Organizational Agent of Change: An

Evaluative Literature Review." *Information Technology and Libraries* 4, no 1 (March 1985):19-20.

Professional Development Program, Rockefeller College of Public Affairs and Policy. *Summary of Recommendations Produced by the Task Force on the New York State Public Workforce in the 21st Century*. Albany, N.Y.: The College, 1989.

Schroeder, Penny. "Implementing the Automated Acquisitions System: Staffing Considerations." *Library Acquisitions: Practice and Theory* 12, no 3-4 (1988):423-429.

Spenner, Kenneth I. "Deciphering Prometheus: Temporal Change in the Skill Level of Work." *American Sociological Review* 48, no 4 (December 1983):824-837.

Managing Experts:
Creating Links Between
Librarians, Users, and Systems

Danuta A. Nitecki

INTRODUCTION

New service opportunities are emerging for reference librarians to utilize their expertise as information handlers in assisting researchers to meet their information needs. Reference librarians have traditionally assisted library users in clarifying their information needs, in designing strategies to translate these needs to retrieve information within the structures of appropriate resources, and in evaluating the results of retrieval processes. A logical extension of the traditional reference functions is to apply the understanding of user needs and of information organizational structures to the organization of user held information. In the past few years, microcomputer-based software packages offer organizational structures utilizing expert systems and database management to possibly facilitate this new function. Managerial questions arise concerning the nature and feasibility of expanding the role of reference librarians to support this added function of assisting experts to manage their information.

In this paper, some observations gained from experience with two projects at the University of Maryland at College Park (UMCP) Libraries which introduced reference librarians and some library users to development of simple expert systems will be shared. Both projects utilized the commercially available expert system software

Danuta A. Nitecki is Associate Director for Public Services, University of Maryland at College Park Libraries.

59

shell, First Class. Both applications of this shell resulted in the fairly limited use of an expert system to direct users to recommended information sources in response to their choices of predetermined menu selections.

The motivation to undertake these projects came from a managerial perspective to consider the feasibility of reference librarians (1) to create an expert system for public use, as part of their routine duties, without major additional staff resources or advanced training, and (2) to provide consultation to select users in organizing their own information sources by utilizing microcomputer-based software, such as an expert system shell.

Both projects were intuitive explorations, not conducted within a formal theoretical or empirical research setting. The results shared here may therefore have limited applications. However, since little guidance on management of reference staff involvement with expert systems was found in the literature, these observations are offered as a case study, hopefully of preliminary interest to those contemplating similar ventures.

The intent in this paper is thus to review briefly both projects, with (1) observations about managerial issues, and (2) reflections on future directions for handling emerging public services. This paper will not describe the details of the content or structure of the pilot expert systems created, nor will it discuss any user evaluations.

BACKGROUND LITERATURE

When the first project was undertaken in 1987, the published literature did not offer guidance on managerial issues of introducing expert system applications to services. Experiences at the National Agricultural Library described by Waters[1] encouraged involvement of reference librarians, but did not focus on the implementation process. There are several articles describing expert systems applications in reference work. A good explanation of expert systems and overview of their development through the mid-1980s is offered by Yaghmai and Maxin.[2] The authors suggest applications of expert systems to information work in several areas, including on-

line database searching, cataloging, and indexing. James Parrott
has authored a few informative descriptions of REFSIM, a knowledge-based reference system developed on a Vax at the University
of Waterloo.[3] From this work on a Vax, several recommendations
concerning design features were made which can have applications
to microcomputer-based system developments. Conclusions and
recommendations about expert system design features are available.
However, a more recent literature review still identified very little
which focused on the managerial issues raised in this paper.[4]

FIRST PROJECT: MANAGING EXPERT
INFORMATION PROFESSIONALS

The first project was a pilot intended (1) to familiarize reference
librarians with an expert system, specifically using First Class,
(2) to involve staff in the exploration of potential applications of
this expert system shell for public services at UMCP Libraries, and
(3) to identify factors affecting reference librarians' ability to design
and create expert systems themselves.

The idea for this project emerged after the author attended a staff
development program conducted by Samuel Waters at the National
Agricultural Library. The short experience offered a good introduction to First Class, a theoretical framework, experience in creating a
small expert system, and some of the sponsor's enthusiasm to see
what applications could be implemented. At the time, at the UMCP
Libraries, there was only spotted general interest in expert systems
among staff. No reference librarian had any experience utilizing an
expert system, no one had an understanding of First Class, and only
a very few had a familiarity with either the concept of a "shell"
application software or with expert systems.

By the end of April 1987, a group of eight reference librarians
volunteered to begin this project. The group of eight met with the
author to set the logistics of the project. Two teams of four each
were formed; before the project's conclusion, one person left from
each team. Each team was given a specific topic for which to develop an expert system. One was to identify how to find a monograph, while the other was to identify how to find a serial. The

teams were to work independently under directions of their chairs. By early summer and again in fall, the two teams met together with the author to share progress reports and exchange feedback on the designs. The remaining schedule was set back. It was clear by this point that the two teams functioned differently and were at different stages of development of their expert systems. In early December 1987 a divisional staff forum was held which included a panel discussion of the project and the future possibilities of expert system applications for reference services. Time for hands-on use of several expert systems was given and participants were asked to evaluate the products of the project. Staff reactions were good, with specific suggestions for improvements. The teams were both proud and encouraged. Afterwards, an evaluation meeting of the teams was held and basic conclusions were reached. A general consensus was that the products should be finalized for use with the public and that more topics should be pursued. Having accomplished the project's intentions, this expert group of staff was invited to serve as an expert system advisory group to continue efforts in this area.

An interesting shift emerged when this group was reconvened the next fall, after other software was discovered. Most significant was the interest among some staff to explore hypertext software, both HyperCard from Apple and Hyperties for DOS-based systems developed on the UMCP campus by Dr. Ben Shneiderman, Head of the Human-Computer Interaction Laboratory. This type of software offers a different approach to organize information. Its flexibility to offer more user interaction promised better solutions to the instructional role many of the participating staff felt was difficult to meet with the expert system shell, First Class. Recommendations broadened the direction of this pilot group's organizational interests. They urged that they be reconstituted, with a few other specialists, to form an advisory group about applications of new technologies in general to developing public services. The need was felt for a staff clearinghouse of information on developments, for a communication focal point, for a planning or priority setting effort, and for an editorial monitor for the quality and public image of various creative products. The details for establishing such a group are being developed.

A. Management Issues

Reflections on this project identified three groups of issues influencing the management questions posed. These include issues of the available resources, the logistics of the assignment, and the participants' interaction.

1. Available Resources

The available resources to the groups included three elements: (a) an "expert" resource person, (b) the software's potential and (c) time.

A resource person was made available to the staff of both groups. This was a library science graduate student who had, herself, designed an expert system using First Class and was taking an independent study to learn more about it. As part of her study, she was to observe the development process. She presented an initial introduction about expert systems to the whole project team, but afterwards it proved too difficult to schedule her participation with the two teams' activities. The general consensus of the participants was that such an "expert" on expert systems was unnecessary. Also most felt that the print documentation and personal consultation available by phone from the First Class producer were quite good.

The First Class software was adequate for the project's intent to introduce staff to expert systems and to develop a single and general-level directional reference aid. However, some participants found that the software potential was limited. It did not allow for more repetitive movement for instructional applications, nor did it allow for easy shifts in the direction of reference advice, to respond to increased clarification of a user's needs. In fairness to the software, however, the group did not exhaustively test the product's potential. Recently an upgraded version has been ordered which incorporates features of hypertext to the expert system's shell.

Time turned out to be more an unknown than a resource. The project was undertaken on a voluntary basis, with no extra personnel resources or release from other duties given to the participants. It was clear that the groups could set their own pace with only a few milestone targets to be reached. A flexible schedule with some slippage did emerge. At the beginning, it was unknown how much time was needed for staff to learn the software and to produce then a product. At the conclusion, staff estimated each spent approximately forty hours to reach a first stage draft product having begun with basically no knowledge of the package. Comments from some staff reflected varied levels of time pressure and constraint. Since this was a learning pilot, an initial effort, it seemed important to complete something first rather than drag development to reach perfection. Some participants noted that the project took far more time than was anticipated and this impression was amplified by the fragmented attention each could give the project. No one had adequate blocks of time to concentrate efforts to complete the project without feeling that some software functions had to be relearned or that only enough of the software was explored in order to satisfy the immediate project need. The constraint of available time was noted to be an inhibiting factor in investigating the software's full potential or experimenting with it to develop more subtle approaches.

2. Assignment Logistics

The logistics of the assignment may have been artificial for a learning experience; however, they were set to focus attention on exploring the software, to consider its application, and to benefit from group support in the learning process. Observations about several factors related to these logistics may be worth considering in managing another learning-production project such as this.

One factor is assigning a topic. The intent of doing so was to focus staff effort on their learning the software and the very concept of an expert system. The topics were easily embodied within each participant's expert knowledge, and thus it was hoped to place each on equal footing in creating the expert system. The two groups responded differently to this condition. One group's members seemed to approach their assignment by dividing the topic by subject discipline. Everyone learned the software and organized a segment of the subject content in creating the expert system. The other group began with the intent that the chair would learn the software and the others would develop the data for input. This proved to be extremely stressful and burdensome on the chair and difficult to accomplish. A shift was made whereby each member developed a portion of the topic. One member describing the results said "they reflected a certain anarchy of approach" requiring editing. In fact the assigned topic was then followed by some and ignored by others. Considerable debate took place whether assigning the topic dampened motivation of the participants since several had different ideas for creating an expert system. If done again, the assignment approach should be kept to a minimum time period to allow participants to learn and practice using the software, and then provide greater freedom to pick one's own topic soon after.

Another factor is the emphasis to create a product. The intent here was to offer a positive, tangible way to understand an expert system and the expectation was that the involvement would raise interest. The two groups functioned slightly differently. From the start, one seemed to organize efforts to complete the product, with early delegation of tasks and group sharing. The other group began with a less explicit plan. The members acknowledged that much of the uncertainty about the best way to proceed began to disappear as more of the system design was put on paper. The logic of the modules changed as they were prepared for input. An observation emerged that the objective to create *something* quickened the transition from the theory and conceptual levels of understanding expert systems to the practical consideration of their application.

Another factor in the logistics is the competitive setting of two groups working independently. The intent of introducing competition was to stimulate creativity in the approach to problem solving. However, the groups' results were relatively free of any sense of competition. The groups worked independently with little time to compare themselves to each other. During the meetings when progress reports were made from both groups, ideas were freely shared and some jointly adopted.

Another factor is the participants' introduction to the expert system concept made at the start of the project. The intent of the introduction was to describe a few applications as illustrations, not to stress any model system, but to make available working examples. The general function of an expert system and a design strategy were suggested. The mechanical steps of how to utilize the software shell were intentionally not included in the introduction. The project feedback was to see if this introduction was adequate. Some felt it would have been helpful to be able to inspect a working expert system for library applications in more depth before starting, while others suspected they might have been influenced by a model's approach, limiting their own exploration.

Finally, a factor of the logistics worth noting is the system production or online work. The production logistics were intentionally left to the teams to determine and undertake. No separate typists were made available to the project. As noted earlier, the groups took different approaches. One shared all aspects among the participants, including typing input online. The other centralized the mechanics of production to the chair until the efforts split among the team members. The initial rationale for the centralized approach was the assumption that if one person knew the software thoroughly and could do all the input, then the others could be free to be "experts" and concentrate on conceptual aspects of the project. In retrospect, the recognized advantage of decentralizing knowledge about the software was that more staff have become prepared to lead others interested in developing expert system applications. The decentralized approach also suggested the role of the chair could be more that of the needed system editor, responsible to link contributions of others with some consistency of approach and style. Most found the actual input to be simple using First Class and, in the future, could be assigned to a typist once the system logic was designed.

3. Participants' Interactions

Much of the process of creating an expert system as illustrated by this project seemed influenced by the nature of the participants' interactions. Two issues especially seemed to affect this: the leadership style and the planning effort.

Totally unexpectedly, the leadership styles of the two chairs did seem to influence their teams' progress and approach to the design of the expert system. Some examples have been noted already. Observations are that one chair's leadership style reflected a gatekeeper who preferred to centralize activities and personally do most of the work. No early decisions were made about strategy to approach the problem. This chair's group expressed more frustration and became more splintered, while the chair quickly showed stress. However, after initial false starts, the group's method did develop one strategy that worked well. One person designed a module and then explained and discussed it with the group chair in conversational fashion. Suggestions were made and the results reflected both persons' perceptions. One participant observed that this was the only way this group could proceed, given differences in personal levels of motivation and difficulties of getting the whole group together at once. The resulting product was a patchwork of different independent efforts.

The other group chair's style was participative. The chair suggested, and others responded, to delegate tasks from the start. More interaction occurred among all members. A similar level of enthusiasm seemed to be maintained by all throughout the project, and although at the start, each had different levels of skills, by the end, similar functional skills emerged. The resulting product is more integrated.

The different manner of interaction among each group's participants may have contributed to their difference in offline planning. The less successful results of the centralized approach pointed to the value of placing a proportionally high degree of effort in the offline planning stage. The decentralized group developed a plan first and spent less time in deciding what to do and how to do it. Suggestions emerged that for any future project, a full day or two should be devoted to designing the expert system's structure and planning the work flow. A planned framework seems clearly to be desirable for expansion or refinement of a system. Time invested in these early, offline steps pays off in total effort.

B. Suggestions for Managing In-House Creation of an Expert System Application

A few suggestions for managing in-house creation of an expert system application emerged from the limited experience offered by this project.

1. *Initiate novice staff.* Give a basic theoretical overview and practical explanation. Emphasize the shell's skeletal function. Demonstrate examples to illustrate potential applications.

2. *Learn by doing*. Expecting a product encourages a quick transition from anxieties of undertaking a new theoretical concept.

3. *Approach group learning exercise as a production project.* Group learning seems to offer support. Set objectives to educate staff and to develop a usable product. Select a chair carefully for leadership qualities. Select a topic for learning expert system concept and software for which expertise is common among staff. Identify audience for whom expertise is useful. Set project with reasonable timeframe, allowing for approximately 40 to 50 hours learning time per person, for milestones to review progress, for user testing and evaluation, and for editing a final usable product. Preferably devote a block of at least two full days of learning time to concentrate on the project.

4. *Designate a system editor.*

C. Suggestions for Creating an Expert System for Public Use

Although this paper's focus is not about the contents of an expert system, a few pointers for staff to consider in its creation might be offered. The literature does report numerous research findings on design elements for creating human-machine interface software, including expert systems applications. This is an area of growing interest and thus a current literature review will likely produce numerous new citations. Harold Borko offers several insights into designing an expert system, including the following:

> It is important to select a task and a program design for an ES project that is neither so narrow as to be trivial nor so general or so complex in nature that the programs become unwieldy and their problem-solving efficiency drops below acceptable levels. . . , heuristic rather than algorithmic search procedures must be employed while recognizing that these may not always lead to an acceptable solution.[5]

He also notes, as recently as in this 1987 article, that

We do not know how to design a true expert system that can be expected to process the breadth of knowledge that is called common sense, that can duplicate intelligent human behavior in all its aspects, or that can reason at the level of expert humans. . . . ES can at best serve as a surrogate consultant to which the user could turn for advice and for aid in solving a very limited set of real-world problems.[6]

One recent article by Borgman, Case and Meadow is helpful in summarizing specific design recommendations based on their own and other related work researching front end user interface design. Among their recommendations are the following:

Knowledge of the subject area and of the use of microcomputers should be assumed and not taught. . . . Users are "bothered greatly" by lack of consistency in screen presentations. . . . Window placement should be used as cue to the information conveyed, with consistency throughout. . . . Users have a preference for interactivity, desiring opportunities to provide input and to receive feedback from the system.[7]

Intuitive conclusions reached by the library staff involved in this learning exercise at UMCP offer a few other practical suggestions for creating an expert system for public service application:

1. Select a shell with adequate documentation for self-learning, with capability to be reproduced within an application, and with telephone technical assistance offered by the producer.
2. Plan conceptual content of the expert system offline as an early step of the development process.
3. Maximize use of existing print aids for expert system content; use content of existing pathfinders where appropriate.
4. Determine approach of expert system's organization with value to the reference librarian's experience with users.
5. Explore full potential of the shell used.
6. Aim to link expert system into an integrated user package; think of modular units.
7. When possible, incorporate educational function by showing

reasoning as well as results in various steps of the expert system's paths.
8. Keep screen display simple and clearly organized.
9. Avoid long, multiple screen narratives.
10. Avoid jargon, abbreviations and acronyms.
11. Minimize number of steps required to reach results.
12. Be sure instructions on navigating through the system are clear.

SECOND PROJECT:
MANAGING USERS' INFORMATION

The second project reviewed in this paper utilized development of an expert system for a different purpose than in the first project. The purpose of this second project was twofold: (1) to identify factors affecting a new library service concept by which a reference librarian offers consulting to patrons on how to organize a body of their information, using a microcomputer-based software; and (2) to compare the usability of an expert system and of a database management software package in navigating users to relevant materials in a collection.

The opportunity to undertake this project was formalized by receipt of a small faculty-librarian research grant from the Council on Library Resources.[8] The project directors proposed to consider these two issues through a small study involving the collection of the Middle Atlantic Region Japanese in Schools (MARJIS) program. Among its many activities, this program, under Dr. Barbara Finkelstein's direction, aims to familiarize high school teachers with a multistate region, with curriculum materials useful in introducing Japanese culture to American students. In support of this function, the UMCP Libraries has temporarily given space to house the MARJIS Clearinghouse where teachers and students gather and use materials from a collection of curriculum materials.

The Council grant supported a small experiment for which one hundred titles from the MARJIS collection were identified by its staff. Brief bibliographic information and a short descriptive annotation for each were written for entry both in an expert system utilizing First Class and in a database management program using Inmag-

ic. The expert system was designed to navigate users through a
series of selected responses to four questions to a recommended
reference source available in the MARJIS Clearinghouse. The questions were determined by the MARJIS staff, based on experience
with how teachers seek curriculum information. The data management program offered access to the same information, but retrieval
was based on the user's identification of relevant keywords, as
tagged from the bibliographic identification and annotations of the
entries. The final evaluation stage of the project is underway, when
Clearinghouse users are asked to use one of the two systems to
identify sources for preselected questions about Japanese culture.
The users are then asked to complete a questionnaire about their
perceptions of ease of use, and their search results will be reviewed
to determine relevance of retrieval in each program. From the experiment, the MARJIS staff hopes to draw conclusions on the best
application of each software and select which to use to complete the
bibliographic control of the Clearinghouse collection. Similarly, the
project should offer insights concerning the Libraries' potential
consulting service whereby reference librarians may assist faculty
to organize information gathered for their research, teaching or service projects in ways that it can be retrieved most easily to meet
their future needs. Although only preliminary discussions have occurred among the project participants and the user evaluation is not
completed, a few key observations that clearly emerged from this
experience can be highlighted here.

These observations will be considered from the concerns of managing a potential consulting service which, if successful, could assist users to create such individualized programs. Three phases of
the service clearly surfaced from the project. These might be re-
ferred to traditional tasks such as: (1) user instruction, (2) the reference interview, and (3) the consultation.

A. User Instruction

User instruction in this context needs to introduce the patron to
the conceptual framework by which information may be organized
for retrieval and by which available software programs function.
This is not a trivial task and is key to the continuation of an effective

dialogue with the user. Although good reference librarians in academic settings describe the organization of reference tools many times each day as they introduce a user to a new source, it is a different perspective to describe how one might organize information to produce one's own reference source. A new vocabulary is needed, much as occurred when librarians incorporated the specific use of "and" "or" "not" to explain Boolean logic to first time machine-readable information searchers. The jargon of information science, of indexing, and now of peculiar software packages needs to be translated into relevant terms for the user. We can assume, incidentally, that this user is not primarily interested in becoming an expert in organizing information, but seeks help to organize his own private information explosion for practical future use. Staff witnessed in the previous project, and here again, how important the introduction of the concepts of these new tools are.

To develop this service, new forms of instructional aids likely will need to be developed. The work with the MARJIS staff on the expert system clearly illustrated the value of using an illustrative example of another expert system to clarify the notions of knowledge sets, and the variable inference rules governing the paths of choice offered a user. Better samples need to be developed to illustrate the potential of these and other software packages to be made available through the consulting service.

B. Reference Interview

During the reference interview the purpose organizing the targeted information and the projected retrieval patterns need to be identified. The development of the MARJIS expert system illustrated very well how the form of reference interview within this new service is perhaps more intense and demands more of the user than a typical dialogue at the reference desk. The purpose here was ultimately to facilitate access to the MARJIS collection of materials to yet another, more remote group of users. This required identification of the targeted users and the degree of user sensitivity expected in the final product. In this case, the primary user group was to be high school teachers and the resulting expert system needed to be self-explanatory and easy to use with minimal or no assistance. The aim was to create a guide which could be distributed to schools for independent use away from the MARJIS staff. Similarly, the identification of projected retrieval patterns was based on the MARJIS staff experience with how teachers ask for information and with curriculum factors affecting their selection of sources. These were identifications the service user (i.e., the MARJIS staff) needed to consider and determine. It required time and collective thinking. In other cases, one may find the service user wishes to closely replicate search habits previously used. In either approach, these search protocols become the basis for either the variables defining the knowledge sets or the rules defining their relationships.

To reach this point in the service process required a merging of expertise. The user understood the potential audiences of the expert system and the factors affecting the way sources are identified by them. The librarian in turn knew the software package potential and the concepts to offer a framework for eventually linking the user and sources via the expert system. The reference communication skills of drawing out parameters of a user's information need and of actively listening are essential. Helpful traits to participate as a librarian in this service seem to include those desirable of all reference staff—to be analytic, communicative, intuitive, systematic and organized. An added demand, however, is to review a software package for this new reference advisory service function. This must be done with compatible equipment. Unlike reviewing a print tool, such review cannot be done linearly from cover to cover, but might best be done with test applications. The need for criteria by which to review applications software emerged as a prerequisite to offering this service.

C. The Consultation

In the consultation the librarian merges typical reference traits including knowledge of sources, experience-based judgment, and personal insights. These are utilized for two parts of the consultation: to recommend appropriate software to meet the user's organization and retrieval needs, and perhaps to offer a production strategy for the user to implement its applications.

The recommendation to use First Class and Inmagic were artificial during this project since participants had a limited familiarity with the range of software options. But for the purposes of the project, they worked well to illustrate some differences. First Class was effective as a means to create limited, but highly directive paths to recommended sources. Inmagic was effective to offer a more user-defined path to recommended sources. The produced expert system seems easier to initially use, but has more restricted search results. The created data management system is more difficult to initially learn to use, but once mastered, offers the user more opportunities to retrieve unanticipated results.

There is some question whether or not to include a recommended production strategy as part of the consultation service, and yet it is critical to have a plan developed for the successful creation of a database or expert system. The question revolves around where to draw the line on the responsibility or accountability the librarian has for the end results. At present it is difficult to foresee having the staff resources to undertake actual production. This project illustrated the need for quality control seen in such steps as consistency in editing, authority control on tagged headings in the data base system, and completion of logical paths in the expert system. Supervisory oversight rested with the user. Although most of the initial intellectual identification of variables and selection of sources were undertaken by two expert faculty members, the data entry was done by several different assistants, working fairly independently and with varied familiarity with the project. As a result, some cleanup and modification needed to be done prior to the patron test. Given the experimental nature and relatively small size of the project's expert system, this was not problematic. But error correction could be an expensive, labor-intensive factor in a larger system creation. The experience of this project brought attention to the need to advise prospective developers of the steps involved, the level of staff attention needed, the estimated time commitment required, and the potential detrimental impact of errors. In short, it is desirable to develop a program, complete with procedures, evaluations, and schedule. The librarian can advise, but unless added resources can be committed to the service, should not undertake a project manager role.

D. Feasibility of Offering
Consulting Service

From the second project's experience, some initial observations are made about the feasibility of offering a consulting service for users to organize their information sources by utilizing microcomputer software.

This project illustrated that it is a doable and desirable service. A librarian was able to introduce two different approaches for a user to organize control over a collection, using microcomputer-based software. The basic structure for two complete access aids to the MAR-JIS collection have been created and the staff hope to utilize both for different functions.

As noted, several resources for such a consulting service to evolve must be developed. These will include at least the following: a collection of relevant software packages; a framework to review applicability and potential of such packages; illustrative examples of the results of using the various packages; prepackaged end user instructions; and a focal service location to include equipment to test software and to consult with users.

All this takes time. Until more reference librarians understand software applications for organizing and retrieving information, managing such a service must factor staff learning time. The reference librarian involved in this project was already very familiar with First Class from participation in the first project described above, and was software literate enough that learning Inmagic was not time-consuming. Estimates are that he spent approximately twenty-five hours working with the user in preparing the Inmagic package. It is assumed that when another consultation is done using similar software, less time will be required.

CONCLUDING COMMENTS

A concluding observation is that the phenomena of utilizing microcomputer-based software by reference librarians has posed a managerial challenge to link traditional missions with creative innovations and to balance evolving service initiatives with available resources. One role of the reference librarian is to connect users to knowledge through navigated access to information. One expert system shell and other microcomputer-based software have offered librarians at UMCP Libraries an entry to broaden their perspective on how to do so beyond traditional in-person reference services.

In particular, from these project experiences, interest has been sparked in two service directions. One is to develop more instructional and directional packages for patron use. Beyond what has been described here, reference staff have begun to explore the Apple HyperCard software for simplifying access to serial bibliographic controls; and a graduate student is working to develop an introduction to the libraries using the Hyperties, DOS-based software. Librarians hope eventually to utilize an affordable authoring system to combine features of an expert system, interactive video, and access to remote files for improved user assistance.

The other direction is to develop a consulting service by which librarians offer use of tools and advice to patrons on developing their own organization of information. The influence of such a service seems far reaching, since many campus researchers not only need to organize information for their own use, but also extend access to others through their research and public services programs.

Such new directions place demands on management and staff. Perhaps the most difficult for some is to be flexible, open to inquiry, and capable of taking risks. Supervisory attitudes incorporating these characteristics may need to be encouraged among library managers.

But in addition, other existing organizational stress points may be pressured to accommodate these directions. Service staff must maintain awareness of new technological and service developments. As a result, more staff development programs might take the form of equipment demonstrations and descriptions of new applications. Access for staff use of various software packages, many not inexpensive, is needed to continue growth of these service initiatives; collection and operations budgets need to be modified to accommodate such growth. Similarly, sufficient facilities are essential; adequate numbers of compatibly equipped workstations are needed for both staff to develop and learn software packages, as well as for patrons to use them. The speed of change in this environment is too rapid not to involve as many staff as can be enticed, assigned, or spared from other duties. This calls for a managerial sensitivity to respond to, and sometimes to create, opportunities, while not overburdening the limited resources available to maintain quality in existing, desirable services. Simultaneously to expanding involvement, a managerial coordination of projects, through effective communication becomes essential. One other managerial demand which has a new slant is that of instilling quality control on public products while not curbing staff initiative. Creative means for oversights are needed.

The impact on staff of exploring new user applications of microcomputer-based software will be affected by the management of such exploration. Some staff will be anxious and apprehensive of the unknown and may require greater educational opportunities. Some library schools have begun to incorporate the required skills to handle expert system design in their curriculum.[9] But many reference librarians who graduated before such curriculum changes were introduced are also excellent candidates to learn and grow from these new applications. The reference librarian who was involved in the consultation project experienced satisfaction in providing a highly individualized and personal information service, seldom affordable in daily reference desk activities. Such a service also can offer professional growth with each implementation, since an overlap of the user's subject expertise and the librarian's information handling knowledge must occur.

Development opportunities are exciting and often are welcome. Staff involved in the two projects described here seemed to make time for the undertakings, even though no spare time seemed to exist in already demanding service assignments.

There is much work to be done among all information professionals in improving library users' abilities to organize and retrieve needed information. Experiences described in these two projects are not meant to suggest that reference librarians alone should expect to undertake the sophisticated research and programming required to develop powerful expert systems. The literature offers many testimonials of significant progress being made by systems designers and computer science specialists to develop such programs, some with and some without benefit of reference librarians' expertise.

These projects have demonstrated, however, that reference librarians, not formally trained as programming specialists, can become involved in this developing area of electronic user assistance. Microcomputer-based software packages, artificially intelligent or dumbly obedient, give reference librarians exciting new opportunities to further explore their service functions and to create innovative products and services to support user information handling needs. These opportunities reemphasize the librarians' role to link the user with knowledge through instruction, direction, and organization. In managing the programs described here to explore these opportunities, automated service initiatives have emerged to incorporate user instruction into expert systems, to create expert pathways for navigating users to sought knowledge sets, and to consider assistance for users to organize better their private information collections. These experimental initiatives are exposed here in their infancy both to invite conversation and to encourage others to participate in this exploration.[10]

NOTES

1. Samuel T. Waters, "Answerman, the expert information specialist: an expert system for retrieval of information from library reference books," *Information Technology and Libraries* 5:3(Sept 1986):204-212.

2. N. Shahla Yaghmai and Jacqueline A. Maxin, "Expert systems: a tutorial," *Journal of the American Society for Information Science* 35:5 (Sept 1984):297-305.

3. From the following descriptions, the involvement of a reference librarian, James Parrott, in designing an expert system at the University of Waterloo is implied. See: James R. Parrott, "Expert systems for reference work," *Microcomputers for Information Management* 3:3 (Sept 1986):155-171; R. David Binkley and James R. Parrott, "A reference-librarian model for computer-aided library instruction," *Information Services and Use* 7:1 (1987):31-38; and James R. Parrott, "REFSIM: A bimodal knowledge-based reference training and consultation system," *RSR Reference Services Review* 16:1-2(1988):61-68.

4. A more recent literature review uncovers several descriptions of other expert systems applications to information work. Those particularly interested in this topic may wish to examine *Information Processing and Management* 23:2(1987), an issue devoted to the topic, or to recent monographs on the topic such as Rao Aluri and Don Riggs ed., *Expert Systems in Libraries*, Norwood, N.J.: Ablex Publishing Corporation, (1990); or Ralph Alberico and Mary Micco, *Expert Systems for Reference and Information Retrieval* (Westport, CT: Meckler, 1990).

5. Harold Borko, "Getting started in library expert systems research," *Information Processing and Management* 23:2(1987):83.

6. *Ibid.* p. 83.

7. Christine L. Borgman, Donald O. Case, and Charles T. Meadows, "The design and evaluation of a front end user interface for energy researchers," *Journal of the American Society for Information Science* 40:2(March 1989):101-102.

8. Council on Library Resources. Faculty/Librarian Cooperative Research Grant (4035). Principal investigators: Barbara Finkelstein and Danuta A. Nitecki, "Evaluation of expert system software application for identification of curriculum information," 1987-88.

9. For further discussions of the implications for library education, see: Harold Borko, "Artificial intelligence and expert systems research and their possible impact on information science," *Education for Information* 3:2(June 1985): 103-104; Michael Brittain, "Implications for LIS education of recent developments in expert systems," *Information Processing and Management* 23:2(1987):139-152; and Anne Morris and Margaret O'Neill, "Information professionals — role in the design and development of expert systems?" *Information Processing and Management* 24:2(1988):173-81.

10. Several people deserve special appreciation for their participation in the projects described here. Samuel T. Waters, Associate Director, National Agricultural Library, was instrumental in introducing the author to the possibility of involving reference librarians in exploring expert systems for library applications. Credit for undertaking the first project goes to the UMCP reference librarians who participated in it: Ray Foster, Martha Hooker, Carleton Jackson, Rebecca (Van Campen) Jackson, Robert Merikangas, and Hugh O'Connor. The second project's activities were primarily undertaken by MARJIS staff, Dr. Barbara Finkelstein and Dr. Anne E. Imamura, and from the Libraries, Ray Foster, Coordinator of Computer-Assisted Reference Services, and the author. This work could not have been undertaken without the general environment of support for exploring new technologies encouraged by Dr. H. Joanne Harrar, Director of Libraries, UMCP Libraries.

Core Competencies:
Recruiting, Training, and Evaluating
in the Automated Reference Environment

Cecilia D. Stafford
William M. Serban

One of the key predicaments of post-industrial society is maintaining a trained work force of specialists capable of responding to rapidly changing technological developments. In all service industry sectors, managers encounter professional staffs with disparate skills, backgrounds, and capabilities. When position vacancies occur, managers face the threefold challenge of recruiting, training, and evaluating new personnel. This raises the question of which competencies are necessary for a highly technical position. Increasingly, managers find themselves in a quandary trying to select a suitable person from a pool of applicants with uneven educational levels, experience, and exposure to the technology. In addition, managers must consider whether to seek a replacement based on the competencies of the former incumbent, or to recruit someone with collateral competencies to enhance overall departmental performance. Finally, it further complicates recruitment when there are severe limits on staff development funds.

Like most service industries, the impact of new technology on libraries is widely recognized. The implications of automation on staff recruitment and development is a topic of occasional research concerning administrators, technical services personnel, or library automation specialists.[1] However, there is little systematic exami-

Cecilia D. Stafford is Head of Reference at the Howard-Tilton Memorial Library, Tulane University, New Orleans, LA. William M. Serban is Assistant Professor of Political Science at Xavier University of Louisiana, New Orleans, LA.

nation of the problems library automation presents to the recruiting, training, and evaluating of reference department personnel. This study seeks (1) to identify the problems new information technology raises for reference librarians, (2) to isolate the specific competencies reference librarians need to cope with new technology, and (3) to suggest strategies for recruiting, training, and evaluating reference personnel in the automated reference environment.

I. THE AUTOMATED REFERENCE ENVIRONMENT

The reference department of today is quite different from the reference department of just a few years ago. The speed of technological advancement in public services librarianship has gained momentum and continues to build. Today a dazzling array of information services utilize a myriad of hardware and software configurations. Despite the fact that librarians frequently fantasize about standardization in technology, the reality of a market economy is that the dog-eat-dog existence of the information technology vendor will probably never allow this to occur. Though it is obvious that a technical services librarian's livelihood depends on his/her ability to become a "near expert" with comparatively few computer systems or products, the typical reference librarian of today faces becoming not only a "Jack of all trades" but a "Master of all!"

With the advent of the 1980s, reference librarians had to focus on only a couple of automated systems. Traditionally these were (1) the library bibliographic utilities such as OCLC, RLIN, or perhaps a local/state network of some kind, and (2) the online database vendor of choice, i.e., DIALOG, BRS, or SDC. Ordinarily the reference librarian had to contend with only one of the bibliographic utilities and one or two database vendors. Reference librarians' use of the bibliographic utilities usually would consist of verifying bibliographic data or searching for external library holdings. Online searching usually would fall under the domain of one or two select reference librarians. It was rare to find an online database searcher who would use more than two vendors.

The issue of training reference librarians in the use of these automated systems reveals a distinct change. On the one hand, with the bibliographic utilities, technical services personnel would receive initial training and, in turn, provide "in-house" training for reference staff to perform the few necessary search functions. Eventually, the reference department supervisor would assume the training responsibilities. More recently, use of bibliographic utilities is typically a part of the on-the-job training virtually all new reference librarians receive who lack exposure to a specific system. On the other hand, administrators did not expect reference librarians to train themselves in the use of online databases. Instead, reference librarians would find themselves in the queue with their technical services colleagues for staff development dollars in order to attend the many workshops vendors offer or to access the number of inexpensive "practice" databases to hone their searching skills.

With the advent of the 1990s, besides the two common types of computer systems in which nearly all reference librarians must develop competence, a host of new "reference enhancers" now appear in many reference departments. Increasingly, users clamor for the benefits of information technology using CD-ROM, OPACs, electronic mail, microcomputer software, microcomputer-compatible statistical files, mainframe-enhanced local databases, hypertext or hypermedia, etc. Not only do the systems themselves vary greatly in use, but equipment needs and search command structures are divergent as well. For many libraries the provision of training in the use of the systems can vary from little to no training at all. Learning to operate these new systems is usually informal or self-taught, often resembling the bibliographic utility model rather than the online searching training model.

One of the most significant new technologies that is having a profound impact on reference departments is the generation of CD-ROM products for a number of heavily used periodical indexes. Not only does the searching command structure for these databases differ from producer to producer, but they employ multifarious hardware as well. With CD-ROM products, the purchaser is solely responsible for the training. This implies that reference librarians themselves must master the labyrinth of hardware, software, and command structures and, at the same time, be ready to instruct end-users in the application of the product. Some librarians have the ability to practice on the system in isolation before introducing it to the public. However many libraries do not have adequate facilities to expedite a "breaking-in" period for the reference staff. Lack of either practice or a sufficient shake down period can lead to poor user service and retard public acceptance of a new system. In some cases, libraries may have a systems development librarian to learn the product and then instruct the reference staff. In other departments which employ several CD-ROM products, training solutions may result from assigning one person the responsibility of acquiring an expertise on a particular service and then instructing the rest of the staff in its use.[2] Although this is a reasonable technique, it places the training burden on the reference librarians. They must find the time to read the manuals (which are not always of high quality), practice the new techniques, and instruct the other staff. Many contingencies such as reference load, staffing levels, or technical acumen can impede the adoption of a new system and can account for variance between libraries in the quality of reference service to support CD-ROM products.

A second major impact on reference departments is the online public access catalogs (OPACs) which replace the traditional card catalog. Although the entrance of OPACs into the reference domain is not new, it is now more commonplace. Again, there are a number of different commercial products available (i.e., NOTIS, DOBIS) and some libraries develop and install "homemade" versions. Frequently, as in other instances already mentioned, reference librarians receive minimal formal training and often resort to (1) rummaging through complicated manuals, (2) consulting the systems librarian or someone in technical services, and (3) practicing continuously in order to discover all of the little "quirks" in the system. Informal surveys indicate that new reference personnel receive OPAC training ranging from highly structured to haphazard depending on the staff development profile of their department. There is no standard or basic form of training even among reference departments employing the same OPAC system.

Another relatively recent development on the automation scene is the use of electronic mail for the receiving and sending of reference questions. Some libraries operate on an inter-institutional basis using such networks as ALANET or BITNET. Others function on an intra-institutional mode taking local queries via communications programs like MUSIC or CMS. Start-up training is generally available through a computer center external to the library for intra-institutional systems. Inter-institutional networks manifest mixed training regimens. After initial training, reference librarians can then instruct one another on the protocols for sending and receiving messages.

Reference librarians frequently incorporate microcomputers for a variety of applications. In a number of libraries, reference librarians assist users in "computer-clusters" or "computer-labs" requiring proficiency in word processors, spreadsheets, bibliography compilers, remote access communications software, relational or statistical databases, etc. Increasing numbers of librarians also operate "computer-assisted instruction" (CAI) activities as part of bibliographic instruction programs. These librarians are frequently responsible not only for the use of the medium, but also for the construction of the programs.

Lastly, a recent innovation in reference automation is the use of hypertext and hypermedia. Hypertext allows the user easy access "... to nonsequential references in literature"[3] while "[h]ypermedia is similar to hypertext, but instead of linking just text, users can link in other media, such as graphics, video, spreadsheets, animations and voice."[4] Libraries use hypertext/media to create such instructional devices as library tours and subject-specific library instruction lessons on computer. Although the use of hypertext/media is not currently widespread in libraries, it is certainly a new use of automation that a number of reference librarians will be facing in the near future. Though formal instruction in the use of hypertext may appear soon, training is currently up to the individual using the medium.

With the proliferation of automated systems and products in reference departments, it is essential for library administrators to look at the people who are staffing these highly technical areas. Who are the people working in these areas? What types of experience, education, and knowledge of computers do these staff members have?

Although the optimal reference staff of experienced, computer-literate librarians is every administrator's dream, this situation does not prevail. Many reference departments have staff ranging from recent library school graduates to senior level members with a substantial number of years of field experience. New graduates may range from highly sophisticated computer users to those with only minimal computer instruction from their library education. The middle and senior level staff may possess the same range of computer expertise, but many of them have had to learn the new technologies haphazardly on the job in an effort to keep up with a rapidly changing profession. All these people, veterans and newcomers, will have to work hard to keep up with the dramatic changes now occurring in automated reference services.

Just as reference departments vary greatly in the computer expertise of their professional staff, departments also vary considerably in the use of support staff. Depending on professional staff size, a library may use support staff to provide reference assistance alongside and sometimes independent of the professional staff. They may range from highly educated and experienced staff to undergraduate student assistants who help keep the reference desk open for public assistance, especially evenings and weekends. The training and supervision of support staff in servicing automated reference products adds a weighty managerial responsibility.

With vastly diversified personnel, what can administrators do to insure that their staffs possess the competencies necessary to provide the best possible assistance in these highly automated reference departments? Can a department guarantee consistency of service no matter who is on duty at any given time during service hours? And if not, how can this be achieved?

II. BASIC COMPETENCIES

According to Webster, competence means "the quality or state of being functionally adequate or of having sufficient knowledge, judgement, skill, or strength (as for a particular duty or in a particular respect)"[5] and "having requisite or adequate ability or qualities."[6] As for the requisite competencies for reference librarianship, there seems to be little agreement.

A number of articles appearing since 1980 discuss competencies for librarians, including Marchant and Smith; Smith, Marchant, and Nielson; Nitecki; and Myers, to name a few.[7] However, the studies by Nitecki and Myers are the only two which address those competencies specifically in automated environments and only Nitecki discusses those competencies for public services librarians.

Drawing from the list of competencies reported in these studies as well as from personal experience, there is a core list of competencies reference librarians need in an automated environment, which include: (1) user/staff interfacing skills, (2) knowledge of traditional and automated reference sources, (3) data retrieval skills, (4) information technology skills, (5) instructional skills, and (6) organizational skills.

User/staff interfacing skills. These include communications skills (both oral and written), human relations skills, analytical skills, job and personal flexibility, and patience. Communications skills are more apparent in the automated environment than in the traditional reference environment. One example is the inability to spell, which can negatively impact the librarian's credibility with patrons when using an automated reference tool. Whereas in traditional printed sources one can browse through the alphabet and not reveal poor spelling skills, the automated tools are frequently unforgiving of spelling errors. Likewise, human relations skills are extremely important in an automated environment. The reference librarian relies heavily on these skills when dealing with either users or staff who may be (1) resistant to using automated sources, (2) arrogant or abusive because they use computers in other capacities, or (3) habitually inattentive to specific computer system protocols. Analytical skills take on added importance when the reference librarian has to decide whether a traditional or automated source is the best tool for a particular question or task. Job and personal flexibility are of paramount importance because the introduction of new computerized sources means that work routines and job requirements change dramatically. A reference librarian who is not flexible will be insecure in a position that is subject to frequent change. The last skill in the user/staff interface is patience. The reference librarian will have to practice a great deal of restraint when dealing with the user or staff who balk at the new technology or the know-it-all who tries to take control of every situation.

Traditional and automated reference skills. After analyzing a user's need for information, the reference librarian must draw against his/her vast knowledge of reference sources. A number of traditional sources do not have computerized counterparts and the reference librarian will have to convey this to the user who insists on using computers for everything. If a computerized counterpart does exist, the reference librarian must know if there are format differences between the two and decide which one is most suitable to the question. For example, there are some CD-ROM products which index only journal literature, whereas the printed counterpart may also index books, technical reports, etc.

Data retrieval skills. Reference librarians should know how to adequately and properly use a computerized source. With automated sources librarians must be especially attentive to the intricacies of the system commands, the indexing terms, and the scope of coverage. Developing optimal data retrieval skills requires constant reviewing of the professional literature and vendor publications. Also, self motivation should indicate a willingness to improve skills in order to maximize the quality of information output.

Information technology skills. This is an area where some of the most significant changes are occurring in reference librarianship. These skills include computer literacy, knowledge of hardware and software, analysis of hardware/software needs, and ability to read and comprehend technical manuals and instructions. Computer literacy is a term that is interpreted in different ways. One dictionary of computer terms defines it as "knowledge of and fluency in computer usage and terminology."[8] This definition seems appropriate to reference librarianship when this fluency and knowledge is specific to the reference context. Reference librarians need to exploit computers fully in reference functions, but they need not be proficient in computer programming/programming languages, unless their specific jobs require that knowledge. The reference librarian must be familiar with the hardware particular automated sources employ. The librarian should be able to use the equipment efficiently and perform simple maintenance tasks. A knowledge of the software is imperative for the librarian to be able to access data from the source. As the reference department continues to automate, the reference librarian should possess the ability to analyze the automation needs of the department in order to select appropriate sources. A proper assessment of automated services will require that the reference librarian read computer journals, specification sheets, technical manuals, and instruction booklets to insure the proper acquisition and use of equipment and software.

Instructional skills. This core competency is becoming more important in the automated reference department. Before the entrance of automated sources into libraries, many users could instruct themselves and others in the application of many traditional reference sources. Reference librarians now instruct users in the operation of a variety of automated tools which, in many cases, are too difficult for the uninitiated user to learn alone. These skills require a clear and concise exposition on the use of computer systems for both individuals and groups. Good instruction of automated sources embodies the ability to explain difficult concepts, handle repetitive questions, and present technical information in a crisp and interesting manner.

Organizational skills. With the proliferation of automated resources, the reference librarian must maintain a number of new files such as licensing agreements, hardware and software documentation, etc. Likewise, reference personnel now handle a variety of new duties and services which require proper organization to provide quick and reliable access. Reference librarians may have to collect fees from users, balance bills from database vendors with log sheets, organize new training programs for users and other staff, and more.

After looking at this list of core competencies, how can administrators begin to identify these competencies in candidates for positions in the reference department?

III. RECRUITING

Recruiting for any library position is a difficult task. In today's automated reference department a well-organized recruitment process is essential. During recruitment, what can administrators do to ensure that candidates can actually demonstrate the core competencies necessary for a reference position?

The first step in the recruitment process is to identify the current automation level of the department, i.e., existence of OPACs, CD-ROM products, or microcomputers. The next step is to look at the department's long-range automation goals. Will the department remain stable with the current level of automation? Are there plans to add databases? Are there plans to purchase more CD-ROM products? Will the department be enhancing the online searching program? The final step is to evaluate the computer competencies of the current staff (see section V, Evaluation, below).

After this departmental evaluation, a manager must assess what level of computer expertise the new recruit should possess. Basically, there are three levels of experts. The first level is that of a computer systems generalist. This is a reference librarian with basic computer skills who is versatile with a number of systems but not expert in a single source. Most entry-level librarians fit this description. A generalist has an ability to orient users to basic computer systems but will not be able to provide in-depth explanations, analyze results, or troubleshoot.

The second type of expert is a selected systems specialist. This is a person who is versatile with several systems but demonstrates wholesale expertise with a single system or systems genre, e.g., the online searcher, CD-ROM specialist, CAI developer, or electronic mail liaison. This person develops a high degree of specialization and acts as the "in-house" expert with whom others consult in problem situations.

Third is an information systems specialist. Increasingly, libraries are dedicating full reference positions to "microcomputer application specialists." These are well-trained information professionals who develop substantial proficiency on all phases of automated reference sources. These librarians understand (1) microcomputers and a variety of software, (2) programming or macro development, and (3) the larger environment of mainframe computers, laser disk technology, and the requisite hardware interfaces.

After deciding which level of computer expertise this position needs, a job advertisement must adequately convey this information. A vague or ambiguous job advertisement can attract candidates who are grossly inadequate or over-qualified for the position. At this time the manager must consider the library's financial commitment to salary and staff development activities. Is the library willing or able to meet the salary demands of a highly skilled automation expert or to supply travel funds for an entry-level librarian who will need extensive training?

After the job announcement, the application process begins. Job applicants typically demonstrate job qualifications through four screening methods: (1) letters of application; (2) resumes or vitas; (3) letters of reference; and (4) personal interviews. The administrator should make sure candidates specifically demonstrate appropriate competencies for the level of the position in the job advertisement. It is important to remember that some of the competencies relate to personal attributes and may be harder to assess.

At the initial application phase, administrators should evaluate the letter of application for good written communications skills which are necessary to perform well in the reference environment. The application process also reveals analytical skills. Those candidates who meet all of the qualifications from the job announcements should indicate in the letter how their qualifications match. An applicant who does not exactly fit all of the announced qualifications should build a case for those auxiliary skills or experiences which might enhance him/her for the position. Candidates may have to prove some of the more ambiguous user/staff interfacing skills during other phases of the application process.

During the review of resumes, administrators should be cognizant that candidates (1) identify traditional and automated reference skills through coursework or experience, (2) list specific software and hardware mastery, and (3) describe instructional skills through bibliographic instruction or teaching experience.

When consulting either written letters of recommendation or personal telephone interviews, administrators should query references about an applicant's data retrieval skills in such situations as proper use of a source in class assignments or in everyday reference work. References can also shed more light on the user/staff interfacing skills such as personal and job flexibility and patience. References can verify information technology skills and assess a candidates level of expertise with computers. Finally, they can confirm organizational skills by commenting on the candidate's ability to meet homework or work assignment deadlines.

During the personal interview with the candidate, administrators and the search committee must focus their observation skills. An alert interviewer can detect virtually all competencies during the face-to-face interview. Telephone interviews are less reliable, but are good preliminary indicators to issues needing follow-up during the on-site interview. Often, candidates can demonstrate user/staff interfacing skills depending on the level of personal interaction. Does the candidate talk disparagingly to support staff or student workers? Is the candidate visibly uncomfortable in the presence of the upper level administration? Can the candidate analyze an automation question and know when to be totally honest or to be tactful? Does the candidate display patience and maintain his/her composure if everything does not come off perfectly during the interview?

The personal interview is also an occasion for the candidate to display a broad knowledge of traditional and automated reference sources listed in the position description. During a tour of the reference area, the candidate can demonstrate appropriate data retrieval skills by describing germane uses of selected reference tools, both traditional and automated. Information technology skills are observable through a discussion of the candidate's background and experience with the software and hardware listed on the resume. The interviewers should watch for candidates who can "talk a good game" on paper, but who cannot answer specific questions about various computer programs, hardware components, or system problems. An applicant gives evidence of instructional skills by answering pertinent questions about experience in teaching situations such as bibliographic instruction. Finally, organizational skills are observable by the way the candidate approaches the interview. If he/she arrives totally unprepared, barring extenuating circumstances, one can assume that this behavior will continue in the day-to-day conduct of the job.

Immediately upon hiring a new reference librarian, the supervisor must observe the newcomer's abilities in the position, prepare an evaluation of how the person fits into the department, and decide if there is a need for further training.

IV. TRAINING

After recruiting a new reference librarian, a certain amount of training will have to take place even if the new person has extensive reference experience. Besides general orientation to automated sources, training is necessary to overcome any core competency deficiencies that the recruitment process identifies.

The reference manager will need to organize an in-service training plan focusing on automation skills for all new personnel. Sheila D. Creth outlines the following steps in planning for training the new employee: (1) analysis of the job, (2) establishment of performance standards, (3) identification of training content and training objectives, (4) determination of training sequence, (5) identification of trainers, (6) choice of training methods, and (7) writing the training plan.[9] Taking an inventory of all automated services and applying it to the above training plan will address training needs.

In addition, new reference librarians should receive encouragement to continue formal technical education and training. Formal education can continue when a librarian wishes to take additional courses at the nearest graduate school of library science or at local extension centers. There are a number of training and education options beyond the continuation of formal library education. These include: continuing education courses; workshops and seminars by library organizations, vendors, local colleges and universities, or corporations; professional readings in library science journals; consultation with colleagues who use the same automated systems; and attendance at professional library conferences which provide opportunities for reference personnel to compare notes, attend workshops, and observe vendor exhibits.[10]

Considering this list of training options, it is apparent that the library must make a commitment, in this time of rapid technological change, to support the continuing education efforts of its reference staff to prevent the stagnation of library skills.

V. EVALUATION

The process of evaluating librarians in the reference environment is very complicated. Much of a reference librarian's work does not lend itself easily to concrete or quantitative measures. Supervisor evaluations, peer evaluations, self-evaluations, and patron evaluations are the four most common ways of determining whether a reference librarian is performing adequately.[11] Obtrusive and unobtrusive observation are other methods for supervisor and peer evaluation. These methods, by nature, tend to be highly subjective and may be influenced by the personal feelings of the evaluator.

It is, however, extremely important to evaluate both individuals and the reference staff as a whole when working in an automated environment. Although deficiencies in information technology skills may not be sole grounds for employee dismissal, it is certainly important to insure that the staff member who lacks these skills is flexible and has enough interest in his/her profession to keep up with the changes in that department.

The best techniques for evaluating the user/staff interfacing skills of the reference staff are personal contact, unobtrusive observation, and user or staff member comments. Communications skills, personal compatibility, job flexibility, and patience reflect in the librarian's interaction with users, staff, and the evaluator. The observation method and comments by the public or colleagues are ways of assessing traditional and automated reference skills. This is also a good way to appraise whether or not the librarian favors traditional sources over automated sources, thereby evincing uneasiness with the use of computers.

Data retrieval skills will appear most often through personal and unobtrusive observation. Other reference staff members may provide useful comments on the librarian's data retrieval skills. Also, user surveys can assist good evaluation, but caution is urged in that all users are not always familiar with the contents of many automated sources and may blame the librarian for system limitations. A general observation on whether or not the librarian seems to know what he/she is doing may be the best survey of the untrained user.

The evaluation of technology skills can employ all three of the aforementioned techniques. Personal and unobtrusive observation should indicate whether or not the librarian under review understands the various hardware and software. Also, users should be able to make general comments on the librarian's ability to combine interpersonal skills and overall familiarity with the various hardware and software in the reference department.

Instructional skills are very obvious through personal and unobtrusive observation. Users make very reliable sources of information on the librarian's aptitude for teaching.

Organizational skills will become apparent to other staff members through day-to-day contact with the librarian. Unobtrusive observation may be less useful in identifying this skill, but users should be able to answer on a survey whether or not the librarian was organized in the delivery of assistance.

After evaluating individual competencies, the manager should construct a personal plan for the new staff person identifying which competencies need more polishing. The department head can discuss these with the individual librarian. Comments and suggestions by both parties should explore the best way to approach the improvement portion of the evaluation.

The next step in the evaluation process is to look at the individual and see how he/she fits into the reference department. Does each individual in the department have coordination duties of automated services? Does every librarian contribute equally in each automated reference activity? If there are coordination duties in the department, the evaluation may call for some rearrangement of these duties. The reference manager may want to undertake this evaluation process with each staff member in the department at the next scheduled evaluation. The entrance of a new reference librarian can sometimes serve as a catalyst for changes that will give new life to the department.

CONCLUSIONS

Today's reference department is undergoing extensive change due to automation. Rather than have the reference staff swept along as powerless observers, administrators can take measures to insure that these librarians have the requisite competencies to function in the automated environment.

Awareness of the growing sophistication in reference automation which this paper outlines is a first step in meeting staff needs. Next is a recognition of the core competencies personnel require in the computerized reference environment. This study suggests six core competencies, but individual departments may discover others. Finally, managers must devise a systematic plan for recruiting, training, and evaluating competent reference librarians with automation skills.

Administrators can insure that all new reference librarians possess the requisite skills or aptitudes. Once recruited, the new reference librarian should receive additional training in areas of weakness and should continue professional development. After initial training, the department head must evaluate the new reference librarian, as well as the other reference personnel in order to correct departmental automation deficiencies. In time reference departments will reach a higher caliber of staff support for automated reference services.

NOTES

1. See Allen B. Veaner, "1985 to 1995: The Next Decade in Academic Librarianship, Part II," *College & Research Libraries* 46 (July 1985); Jon Drabenstott, "Library Automation and Library Education," *Library Hi Tech* 5 (Spring 1987); Debora Shaw, ed., *Human Aspects of Library Automation: Helping Staff and Patrons Cope* (Bethesda, Md.: ERIC Document Reproduction Service, ED 279 333, 1986).

2. Sandra L. Tucker, Vicki Anders, Katherine E. Clark, and William R. Kinyon, "How to Manage an Extensive Laserdisk Installation: The Texas A & M Experience," *Online* 12 (May 1988):39.

3. Karen E. Smith, "Hypertext-Linking to the Future," *Online* 12 (March 1988):33.

4. Ibid.

5. *Webster's Third New International Dictionary Unabridged*, Philip Babcock Gove, ed. (1986), s.v. "competence."

6. *Webster's Ninth New Collegiate Dictionary*, Frederick C. Mish, ed. (1983), s.v. "competence."

7. Maurice P. Marchant and Nathan M. Smith, "The Research Library Director's View of Library Education," *College & Research Libraries* 43 (November 1982):438; Nathan M. Smith, Maurice P. Marchant, and Laura F. Nielson, "Education for Public and Academic Librarians: A View From the Top," *Journal of Education for Librarianship* 24 (Spring 1984):234-235; Danuta A. Nitecki, "Competencies Required of Public Services Librarians to Use New Technologies," in *Professional Competencies-Technology and the Librarian* ed. by Linda C. Smith (Urbana-Champaign: Graduate School of Library and Information Science, University of Illinois, 1983), p.44; Margaret Myers, "Personnel Considerations in Library Automation," in *Human Aspects of Library Automation: Helping Staff and Patrons Cope.* ed. by Debora Shaw (Bethesda, Md.: ERIC Document Reproduction Service, ED 279 333, 1986), pp. 42-43.

8. Jerry M. Rosenberg, ed., *Dictionary of Computers, Information Processing, and Telecommunications* (New York: John Wiley & Sons, 1987), p. 117.

9. Chris Sugnet, ed., "Education and Automation—Present and Future Concerns," *Library Hi Tech* 5 (Spring 1987): 109.

10. Sheila D. Creth, *Effective On-the-Job Training*. (Chicago, Il.: American Library Association, 1986), p. 49.

11. Terry L. Weech, "Who's Giving All Those Wrong Answers? Direct Service and Reference Personnel Evaluation," *The Reference Librarian*, no. 11 (Fall/Winter 1984): 118-120.

Is Library Automation Producing a New Kind of Manager?

Lewis D. Cartee, Jr.

INTRODUCTION

Computer-based technology has become a fact of life, spawned both by the impressive increases in the performance, reliability, and memory capacity of silicon chips and by the dramatic decline in the cost of computing. The library world has embraced this new technology more successfully than many other fields, and most libraries today are using some automated product or service. In 1988, 95% of ARL institutions reported using one or more of the bibliographic utilities for cataloging and 79% had operational online catalogs.[1] The installation of automated systems continues at a healthy pace, with vendors reporting 55% and 16% increases during 1987 and 1988, respectively.[2]

The consequences of automation for library work and workers are apparent. Automation has affected not only the content and distribution of jobs, but has also created some entirely new types of work, prompted some redefinition of functions, influenced interpersonal relationships and job roles, and had repercussions for organizational structure.[3] While automation is changing the library community at such a rate that trends may be difficult to discern, the question is whether it is transforming the academic library manager.

The introduction of information technology has forced library managers to confront several issues, and the solutions suggest that a

---

Lewis D. Cartee, Jr. is the Systems Librarian at Tulane University, New Orleans, LA.

99

new kind of manager is indeed emerging in libraries.

- How can management decisions regarding automation implementation be made so that the costs are minimized, the corresponding rewards maximized, and both costs and rewards are equitably distributed among managers, librarians, and support staff?
- How should management respond to the trend toward more concern with the quality of work life, alongside the library's traditional productivity concerns?
- How can library managers best comprehend, shape and take control of the changes associated with library automation, rather than simply viewing them and their consequences as inevitable?

Examining the areas of fiscal management, human resources management, organizational structure, decision making, and leadership to see how libraries are answering the questions, this paper will maintain that automation is indeed producing a new kind of manager.

FISCAL MANAGEMENT

The skilled management of their institutions' time and money has become a major challenge to library managers confronted by automation. As Allen Veaner predicted just four years ago, the proliferation of automated systems has begun to shift library expenditures from expensive library materials to even more expensive information technologies which require constant attention to capital accumulation and expenditure.[4] Automated systems have never resulted in a reduced total cost of library operation. In fact, they generate their own additional expenses: rising telecommunications costs, a shrinking shelf life for hardware, accelerating user demands for access to the library's database, complex and expensive local area networks to support that access, software requiring frequent replacement to keep systems up-to-date, and training for new users and retraining of personnel whose jobs have been displaced by the new automated systems.

Library managers are aware of the importance of communicating to their administrators and users the increasing costs of automated systems and services. They must now become conscious of the growing urgency to broadcast the benefits as well. Malcolm Getz recently calculated the service benefits resulting from the availability of Vanderbilt University's online catalog, and, as fiscal constraints become more stringent, library managers should anticipate increased demands for this sort of accountability.[5] It is clear that managers must improve their procedures for collecting data on the quantity and quality of the services which their libraries provide, whether by user surveys to assess the library's performance or by evaluating specific library services (interlibrary loan, online search services, circulation, etc.). Over time, data from either of these methods would provide evidence of change in the quality of library services and would build a foundation upon which future improvements in the delivery of library services might be built.

A limited number of funding options are available to support library automation, and the option selected has direct implications for the library manager. Direct funding from the parent institution offers the advantage of flexibility but the disadvantage of potential hostility from the user community. Faculty may resent the diversion of already shrinking book funds to automation, particularly if they are unable to see a direct utility for themselves in the automated system. The library manager must vigorously promote the advantages for users that arise from automation in order to counter this potential hostility, and in recent years we have seen some innovative promotional concepts employed by libraries. External funding options (grants and contracts) tend to reduce the library manager's flexibility and usually bring additional reporting requirements to the funding agency and the parent institution. The automation project may have to be redesigned to meet specific requirements of the funding agency, and the manager may endure new pressures to meet deadlines for delivery of the automated services. Despite these potential difficulties, the number of grant applications for automation projects is rapidly increasing as library managers scramble for their share of dwindling resources.

HUMAN RESOURCES MANAGEMENT

> The reality of the computerized workplace . . . is that the vast majority of employees are expected to carry out routine, repetitive, uninteresting, and alienating chores day after day.[6]

The accelerated rate of change caused by automation and new technologies has affected personnel management in libraries, requiring managers to examine hiring practices, staffing patterns, job analysis, and continuing education. Library managers now seek support staff and student employees who are enthusiastic about working with computers. Newly-hired professionals and supervisors are now expected to have previous experience with computer-based systems.

Designing jobs that will increase productivity and maintain employee motivation and job satisfaction is currently a major challenge for library managers and will likely remain so in the future. Modern job design is the process of specifying the contents of the job, the procedures and equipment to be used, and the relationship to other jobs. Automation traditionally has focused job design on task segmentation—dividing and subdividing of jobs—and too often it resulted in rigidly structured, repetitive jobs. The improving capabilities of automated systems are increasingly transferring decision-making once handled by experienced employees to systems software. Library managers must learn how to design jobs which circumvent both of these distressing trends, and, in doing so, they should keep in mind some principles of modern job design and quality of work life (QWL).

Mark Levine[7] and other writers have listed several predictors of QWL:

- the degree to which supervisors treat subordinates with respect and have confidence in their abilities;
- variety in daily work routine;
- challenge of work;
- extent to which work leads to promotion and good future work opportunities;
- self-esteem;
- extent to which employees' personal life affects office performance;
- whether the work contributes to society;
- job responsibility and authority;
- participation in decision-making;
- autonomy, discretion in setting standards, and development of a sense of responsibility for the work;
- expression of creativity.

Although the professional literature reflects a current interest in QWL, its principles may not be understood and are often misused.[8] For most library managers the consideration of QWL principles in job redesign for an automated work environment is still a new concern. However, there is a growing realization today that managers must find ways to involve staff in automation-related decisions because the success of their automation endeavors are increasingly dependent on how well they understand and employ these principles. Management may address these concerns through careful planning and the formulation of policies which acknowledge employees' concerns and complaints about the new technology. Such policies will allow the library director to let middle managers and staff know that the policies are a serious attempt to improve the quality of working life.

The policies should provide for differences in capabilities among employees. Middle managers and supervisors must learn to trust the employees' own perceptions of what they can accomplish and accept that there are limits to how much a worker can do at a terminal.[9] Management must try to build a degree of challenge into every job. Many library jobs can be made more challenging if the employees are asked to contribute to the automation project through regular discussions with managers, redesigned work flows, or regularly scheduled learning and training sessions. While automation will likely enhance some jobs and make them more satisfying, particularly for professional and technical staff, in other cases it will diminish many satisfying work elements and leave employees feeling robbed of valuable, and still marketable, work skills.

Many library managers still view automation as a means of improving staff productivity. Supervisors and middle managers ought to "abandon the idea that productivity is a measurable quantity and that the manager's job is simply to increase it."[10] Managers should encourage imagination, creativity, and innovation, as well as output. Productivity may be increased, temporarily, by creating narrow, specialized jobs designed around the capabilities of the system. In the long term, however, this approach can actually reduce productivity as decreased employee satisfaction, resentment and stress lead to unacceptable levels of error rates, absenteeism, and turnover.[11] The enlightened library manager realizes that jobs are only as stupid as they are set up to be.[12]

Automation has presented a host of human resources challenges to library managers, including the training and retraining of employees, individual job design, work-unit reorganization, career planning, and providing career path opportunities. Managers are beginning to recognize the value of using quality of work life principles in their approach to these vital employee relations and organizational development problems. In the process, they are learning to encourage imagination, creativity, and innovation, as well as output. Until they successfully grapple with these, libraries cannot realize the full potential of their investment in the new technologies.

ORGANIZATIONAL STRUCTURE OF LIBRARIES

As automation alters the library's environment, managers are trying to work within shifting organizational structures. The library's external organizational relationships have expanded to include: new types of local, regional, and national networks; vendors of products and services engendered by the new technologies; participation in joint projects (and even merger) with the campus computing center; and changing expectations of campus administrators and library users. Libraries are increasingly being asked to play a role in university-wide planning, telecommunications policy making, and allocations decisions for information networks and services because of the cost of these services.

The library is undergoing internal transformation in its technical procedures, workflow and workload, and assignment of personnel. Reassignments are made in the number and level of staff as the volume of original cataloging continues the decline begun with the advent of the bibliographic utilities. The conventional management division between public and technical service operations, and even among the various technical service units, has become blurred because the online systems integrate so many functions. For example, the integrated library systems now permit selectors to perform preorder searching and to initiate purchase orders directly, reducing the workload of acquisitions staff. Some librarians and library managers welcome the breakdown of these traditional barriers and view the new communication and coordination among departments and branch libraries as a healthy development. Several authors have addressed how managers are coping with these changes and what trends may be developing.

Cline and Sinnott, in their 1983 study of the effects of automation on the organization of university libraries, note the emergence of task forces and project committees and speculate that libraries will adopt a form of matrix management.[13] A matrix organization uses temporary groups which cut across traditional structure in order to make decisions and solve problems. The matrix approach also allows for greater power equalization among staff and increased participation. One writer has suggested the development of "hexagon-like" structures (e.g., those with multiple relationships among positions) to accommodate the new technologies.[14] Today most large libraries are using some form of matrix structure.[15]

Other structural options are also emerging in the automated library. Cargill observes that the hierarchical structure is flattening and that the organization may revolve around functions or programs. Functions will merge within positions, and technical and public services staff may find themselves reporting to one senior administrator.[16] For example, as the workload of acquisitions and original cataloging is diminished by automation, libraries may reorganize around the concept of subject specialists who would be responsible for a collection's management and use, including selection, preorder searching, ordering, cataloging, and reference services.[17]

Organizational structure is further complicated by the new external relationships engendered by automation. Automation has introduced new organizational ties for libraries, with database vendors, book and serial vendors linked by computer to the library, computer hardware and software vendors, library networks, and university computing centers. Management's responsibility for maintaining relationships with these outside organizations often cuts across departmental lines within the library, creating what Cline and Sinnott labelled "boundary-spanning roles."[18] These roles are nothing new to libraries. Bibliographers have long been formally linked to faculty, acquisitions staff to book vendors, technical services staff to OCLC and their network provider, and reference staff connected to their counterparts at other libraries. Automation has thrust even more staff, particularly managers, into boundary-spanning positions. Cline and Sinnott observed that "those who play boundary-spanning roles become the primary source of information about their particular environmental area. They are also largely responsible for a library's visibility within the information community."[19] The boundary spanners attain autonomy and power from the accelerating rate of change in libraries. By virtue of their function as a filter and interpreter of information, they may exercise an inordinate control over the dissemination of information within the library. Boundary spanners are more likely than other library staff to influence future developments. Their status is further enhanced by their capacity to insure that developments are consistent with the interests of the library.

The extent to which automation changes the library's formal organizational structure depends upon the administrator's position on automation. Some administrators view technology as a tool to fit into the library's existing structure, while others look upon the introduction of automation as an opportunity to wholly restructure the organization. Both of these propositions are valid, and the extent to which one approach or the other is taken depends upon several factors, including the nature of the institution, the characteristics of the library staff, the disposition and leadership of the library administration, the expectations of users, and the resources which are available. Consequently, a recent survey of library directors supports the view that the profession has not yet arrived at a consensus about the new organizational structure.[20] Radical changes, such as the merging of the library and computing center, may occur only where all of the environmental factors (institutional, political, technical, and human) for such a merger are logical.[21] Martin predicts that the library of the future will have a new organizational structure *only if* the introduction of technology parallels the administration's desire to make a particular change. The fluctuating organizational structure, the increasingly obscure distinctions between library divisions, and the expanding role and influence of the boundary spanners will all continue to occupy library managers' thoughts. Whether they adopt matrix management or a radical organizational restructure, no two institutions are alike, and no two libraries will embrace the same solution. Library administrators should be innovative and must determine for themselves and their institutions the best approach to take.

MANAGEMENT DECISION MAKING

Management decision making might be described as choosing among a set of equally undesirable alternative courses of action. If any single alternative were clearly favorable, the choice would be made by someone subordinate to the manager. The manager will turn toward intuitive decisions if given too much data or data which has not been analyzed and interpreted. The best decisions are made by the managers who have just the right amount of sound information available at the right time. The essence of good management, then, is good information, and "management as a function can be defined as interpretation of information so that appropriate decisions can be made."[22] Rush describes three components of the manager's role: (1) *planning* or setting the organization's course through the definition of purposes, goals, and objectives, (2) *monitoring* of critical data sources to ensure that the organization remains on course, and (3) *controlling* the direction (through decision making) in the face of internal and external influences.[23] Successful management requires continual execution of all three of these primary functions, and it also demands that they be performed within acceptable time frames.

As the arrival of technology has dramatically augmented the services offered by libraries, the expanding dimensions and complexity of library operations has meant that managers need an effective system to supplement the information acquired through direct observation. They require access to increasingly accurate, timely, and complete data to plan, budget, staff, set standards, define policies and procedures, control the influence of unanticipated changes in operations and the environment, and evaluate performance and results. Automation support for management also eliminates the tedium of manual calculations and report preparation, freeing the manager to make more effective decisions. Management information systems are designed to provide that supplemental information, bringing in data from operations, from the library environment (including users), from computations on other data, and from models. First, a good management support system provides maximum support for data gathering, analysis, and synthesis. Second, it provides managers with tools to operate on and manipulate data. Statistical and financial analysis, trend analysis, projections, modeling, plan generation and maintenance, and reporting and record keeping are major elements of such a set of tools. Finally, it must provide these services at times and within time periods which permit management actions to be most effective. Hawks notes that "decision making has become such a critical part of everyday library management that systems are now being designed with management information components from the very beginning."[24] While these systems provide data reporting capabilities on collection development, acquisitions, serials, cataloging, the online catalog, and circulation which can enhance library management, in truth the systems developed to date provide but a rough framework of the management information system.

Today there are computer systems with more than adequate power and storage capacity to facilitate building a good, easy to use, economical management information system, tailored to library managers. That such a system has not already been developed may be evidence that managers would not make effective use of

management information systems if they did become available.[25]
There are factors apparently inherent in the managerial style of academic library administrators which raise serious doubts about
whether libraries will develop such systems and whether managers
will use them.

McClure and Samuels cite two reasons for managerial resistance
to library management information systems. First, librarians' focus
on information itself is typically operations oriented rather than decision oriented. They primarily use computers to solve operations
problems, not to generate management information. Library administrators preclude broad participation in the decision making process.[26] Some obvious potential sources of input for decision making, such as continuing education, past experience, and empirical
research, have *not* been found to be important factors in decision
making. Academic librarians and administrators rely on oral consultation with their peers, either individually or within committee
structures, and ignore paraprofessionals as "meaningful sources of
'professional' decision-making information."[27] Managers often rely
upon a handful of internal information sources for all of their decisions, whether or not those sources are actually qualified to provide
such information. This discourages both the search for alternate information sources and the evaluation of the traditional and alternative sources selected.

The "closed" nature of academic library decision making is further illustrated by library managers' lack of consultation with users.
This failure to consider user input has some critical implications for
academic libraries and their managers:

- Academic libraries are failing to make both an accurate assessment of users' needs and a reliable evaluation of the extent to
  which information services are meeting those needs.
- Libraries are maintaining existing services on the assumption
  that they do meet users' information needs.
- Development of new information programs and services is
  limited, with libraries placing their emphasis on collection
  building and bibliographic control.
- Libraries lack the ability to promptly and effectively react to
  changing environmental conditions, such as revised institu-

tional missions, curriculum changes, and widespread use of microcomputers.[28]

Smart managers recognize that they must improve the quality of decision making if academic libraries are to remain effective in the information age. The planning, monitoring, and controlling functions of management require good information on which to base decisions, and librarians must broaden their sources of information to include users and empirical research. Library administrators should consider how different management styles will increase access to and use of information for decision making. Finally, a concerted effort should be made to develop management information systems and decision support systems in academic libraries. Only then will library managers be able to confront and resolve users' information needs and obtain full productivity from staff members.

LEADERSHIP

Societal changes, advances in technology, and other external environmental modifications are directly affecting the configuration of libraries and their services. Unquestionably, a day-to-day type of leadership is not sufficient to move our libraries into the 21st century.[29]

Library managers have been sorely tested in recent years, by their staffs who have demanded greater autonomy and participation in decision making, by users who have asked for new kinds of services, and by rising operations costs and shrinking resources. The automated library environment, with its attendant changes, has exacerbated these problems and placed new demands on the library manager. A critical responsibility of the manager, particularly in an automated library, is to identify for the staff where the library is going, evaluate the alternative paths for getting there, implement plans which will insure that the goal is reached, and analyze the degree of success that has been accomplished.[30] Effective management alone is no longer adequate to meet this responsibility. There are specific leadership qualities which must be sought and nurtured in library managers if they are to manage the automated environment.

The manager must articulate and maintain a vision of the library's future which can be assimilated by the library's staff. The staff need to share this vision and understand the relationship of their individual job responsibilities to the achievement of the library's goals. The manager's ability to inspire trust in the future of the organization and to encourage commitment and loyalty to the library's mission is crucial if the employees are to feel that their contributions are valuable.

The effective manager in today's automated library should act as a role model for library staff, earning their respect and trust by demonstrating a commitment to the common good, rather than to individual or career goals. Recognizing that personnel is the most valuable resource in the library, the manager will, by his example, encourage staff to reach for higher levels of achievement and to engage in problem solving.

Today's leaders must demonstrate flexibility in their management styles and be willing to explore new and more participatory organizational structures. They must shift from a competitive to a collaborative approach to planning and decision-making—an approach which focuses on the contribution that each individual can make toward the greater good.[31] Managers should seek to create an entrepreneurial spirit throughout the management group. They must be willing to explore new ideas and how the ideas might be adapted before they are critiqued and dismissed.

Effective managers and leaders need to take calculated risks to achieve their vision of the library, but risks should not be taken blindly. Cargill cites these steps which should be followed by a good manager before taking a major risk. First, a careful evaluation of the situation must be made, including the staff strengths and weaknesses to determine how to effectively use both. The manager will assess the attitude of the parent institution's administration to determine its willingness to support a new approach. A strategy for the proposed change must then be designed which includes alternatives. The smart manager will seek to learn from colleagues in other libraries who have tried similar proposals what pitfalls to avoid and what successes to anticipate. There will be both opposition and support when any venture promising change is undertaken. The manager should anticipate where the opposition and support will likely arise, seeking to maximize the support and minimize, or convert, the opposition. With any risky enterprise exists the possibility of failure, and the manager should examine the consequences of failure and determine if the organization and the manager can endure them. If failure occurs, the manager will determine why, learn from it, and move on.[32]

Progressive library managers are looking at strategic planning as a framework for dealing with the environmental constraints placed on libraries by the development of new information technologies.[33] Strategic planning involves the setting of goals, based upon the organization's mission statement, and the objective evaluation of alternative paths by which those goals can be realized. It requires that managers focus on the broad intentions of the library and its allocations of resources rather than upon an incremental projection of current operations into the future. Charles Lowry views strategic planning as a frame of reference which both allows managers to analyze future obstacles and opportunities and offers alternative courses of action for their consideration. While the library director ought to play a dominant role, the planning process utilizes team decision-making, and other managers and staff are encouraged to participate. The intent of strategic planning is to consolidate resources in the very areas that will make a significant difference in the library's future role, its performance, and its capabilities.

Library automation has provoked the need for a change in management style toward one of leadership which incorporates formulating a vision, serving as a role model, maintaining flexibility, and taking risks. Strategic planning serves well as a tool for remodeling management style to fit automation.

CONCLUSIONS

Library managers must be willing to take some innovative approaches to fiscal management. No longer are libraries merely automating their internal operations. They are providing access to a broad range of new information services and technologies, and the increasing demand for these more sophisticated systems and services will require large sums of money. As resources diminish, the library manager must recognize the call for fiscal accountability. Today's library managers must be conscious that the "people issues" associated with automation have significant short- and long-term implications for organizational effectiveness and quality-of-work-life objectives. There is no single correct approach to these issues, and library managers must develop strategies which are appropriate to their organization's culture and stage of technological development.

The hierarchical structure of yesterday's libraries has become obsolete as the relationships between managers and workers have become more reciprocal. Today's library manager understands that workers expect more influence in the decision-making process, and the manager must be willing to explore organizational structures which allow broader involvement by staff.

If managers are to effectively manage their libraries today and forcefully lead their organizations into the future, they must begin to change the ways in which management decisions are made. Formal mechanisms or systems must be established for the collection, organization, and analysis of information which will support effective management decision making.

The introduction of technology has been accompanied by an unstable, unpredictable environment which is not suited to traditional short-term management strategies. Successful managers must be leaders who can focus a vision, however imperfect, of tomorrow's library and who are willing to assume calculated risks to realize that vision. They must be able to anticipate challenges and devise creative strategies for meeting them.

The turbulent environment of automated libraries will not soon end. In fact, the emergence of new information technologies guarantees that it will remain unstable for years to come. The future viability of libraries and librarianship depends upon the ability of library managers to anticipate and evolve with their changing environment. This paper has illustrated the areas most in need of managerial attention and evolution: fiscal management, human resources management, organizational structure, management decision making, and leadership. Today, library managers are beginning to explore creative approaches and solutions in each of these domains.

Their success portends the emergence of a new kind of manager who will lead the libraries of tomorrow.

NOTES

1. *The Automation Inventory of Research Libraries, 1988,* (Washington: Office of Management Services, Association of Research Libraries, 1988), p.III-14 and III-5.

2. Robert A. Walton and Frank R. Bridge, "Automated System Marketplace 1988," *Library Journal,* 114:41 (April 1, 1989).

3. Alan F. Westin, Heather A. Schweder, Michael A. Baker, Sheila Lehman, *The Changing Workplace: A Guide to Managing the People, Organizational, and Regulatory Aspects of Office Technology* (White Plains, NY: Knowledge Industry Publications, 1985) p.2-8.

4. Allen B. Veaner, "1985 to 1995: The Next Decade in Academic Librarianship, Part II," *College & Research Libraries* 46:301 (July 1985).

5. Malcolm Getz, "Some Benefits of the Online Catalog," *College & Research Libraries* 48:224-240 (May 1987).
Malcolm Getz, "More Benefits of Automation," *College & Research Libraries* 49:534-544 (November 1988).

6. Craig Brod, *Techno Stress: The Human Cost of the Computer Revolution,* (Reading, MA: Addison-Wesley Publishing Company, 1984) p.27.

7. Mark Levine, James Taylor, and Louis Davis, "Defining Quality of Work Life," *Human Relations* 37:100 (January 1984).

8. Charles Martell, "Automation, Quality of Work Life, and Middle Managers," *Library Administration & Management* 1:135 (September 1987).

9. Brod, *Techno Stress,* p.171.

10. Ibid., p.175.

11. Westin and others, *The Changing Workplace: A Guide to Managing the People, Organizational, and Regulatory Aspects of Office Technology,* p.5-2.

12. Brod, *Techno Stress,* p.175.

13. Hugh F. Cline, and Loraine T. Sinnott, *The Electronic Library: the Impact of Automation on Academic Libraries* (Lexington, MA: Lexington Books, 1983) p.131-132, 174-175.

14. Robert M. Mason, "Micros, White Collar Workers & the Library," *Library Journal,* 109: 2133 (November 15, 1984).

15. Duane E. Webster, "Impact of Library Technology on Management," *Conference on Integrated Online Library Systems, September 23 and 24, 1986, St. Louis, Missouri, Proceedings* ed. David C. Genaway (Canfield, OH: Genaway & Associates, 1987) p.175.

16. Jennifer Cargill, "Automation and the Change Process: The Human Factors," *Conference on Integrated Online Library Systems, September 23 and 24, 1986, St. Louis, Missouri, Proceedings* ed. David C. Genaway (Canfield, OH: Genaway & Associates, 1987) p.197-218.

17. Cline and Sinnott, *The Electronic Library: the Impact of Automation on Academic Libraries*, p.174-175.

18. Ibid., p.169.

19. Ibid., p.169.

20. Bessie K. Hahn, Carolyn Gray, and Stuart Langton, "Human and Organizational Issues of Technological Change: An Administrative Perspective," *Conference on Integrated Online Library Systems, September 23 and 24, 1986, St. Louis, Missouri, Proceedings* ed. David C. Genaway (Canfield, OH: Genaway & Associates, 1987), p.293-311.

21. Susan K. Martin, "Library Management and Emerging Technology: the Immovable Force and the Irresistible Object," *Library Trends* 37:374-382 (Winter 1989).

22. J. Michael Bruer, "Management Information Aspects of Automated Acquisitions Systems," *Library Resources and Technical Services* 24:339 (Fall 1980).

23. James E. Rush, "Microcomputers in Libraries: Present Status and Future Trends" in *Microcomputers for Library Decision Making: Issues, Trends, and Applications* ed. Peter Herndon and Charles McClure (Norwood, NJ: Ablex, 1986), p.242.

24. Carol Pitts Hawks, "Management Information Gleaned from Automated Library Systems," *Information Technology and Libraries* 7:133 (June 1988).

25. Rush, "Microcomputers in Libraries: Present Status and Future Trends," p.244.

26. Charles R. McClure and Alan R. Samuels, "Factors Affecting the Use of Information for Academic Library Decision Making," *College and Research Libraries* 6:484 (November 1985).

27. Ibid., p.494.

28. Cline and Sinnott, *The Electronic Library: the Impact of Automation on Academic Libraries*, p.495.

29. Donald E. Riggs, "Transformational Leadership and the Electronic Academic Library," *Conference on Integrated Online Library Systems, September 23 and 24, 1986, St. Louis, Missouri, Proceedings* ed. David C. Genaway (Canfield, OH: Genaway & Associates, 1987), p.366.

30. Charles R. McClure, "Library Managers: Can They Manage? Will They Lead?," *Library Journal* 105:2389 (November 15, 1980).

31. Webster, "Impact of Library Technology on Management," p.183.

32. Jennifer Cargill and Gisela M. Webb, *Managing Libraries in Transition* (Phoenix: Oryx Press, 1988), p.68-69.

33. Charles Lowry, "Convergence of Technologies: How Will Libraries Adapt?" *Library Administration & Management* 2:82 (March 1988).

"We Have a Computer":
Administrative Issues in the Relations Between Libraries and Campus Computing Organizations

Donald J. Waters

Arno Penzias, a vice-president for research at AT&T Bell Labs and a Nobel prizewinner, lucidly describes in *Ideas and Information* his close encounters of various kinds with the contemporary world of "information work." At one point, he recounts his disappointment upon learning that a part he was ordering from a catalog could not be shipped until the next week. But, he complained to the clerk handling his order, the catalog promises same-day service. "You must have a very old catalog," came the response. Without a trace of irony, the clerk informed him: "Now we have a computer."[1]

For an individual or organization to "have a computer" is to experience how deeply automation embeds — some might say entangles — one in a web of complex and interdependent roles and relationships. The web includes, to mention only a few of the possibilities, equipment designers and manufacturers, software engineers and programmers, documentation specialists, product vendors, service agents, and machine operators, as well as one's colleagues, supervisors and clients in the work that is being automated. Of course, in any computer-based automation project, the computer itself is prominent and tends to symbolize either the promise of success — that products or services will increase in quality or improve in quantity — or, as in the case of the mail-order house, the curse of failure. But the computer, by itself, simply does not ac-

Donald J. Waters is Head of the Systems Office in the Yale University Library, New Haven, CT.

count for the success or failure of an automated system. The true gauge, instead, is found in an understanding of the nature, content and organization of the various roles and relationships implicated in the automation web.

Because the roles and relationships are so complex, the points of possible failure so many, and the potential for highly leveraged change so far-reaching, the risks and costs of computer-based automation projects typically are high and require careful management. In college and research libraries, the risks are no less and, in a time of broad and rapid automation, considerable attention needs to be paid to a variety of administrative issues both within the library and external to it. The internal issues include structuring and re-structuring library work patterns, matching existing library staff to new patterns of work through training and reorganization, recruiting appropriately-qualified personnel, and adjusting management styles and focus, including the development of effective forms of salary administration and performance evaluation. Many of these challenging subjects are explored elsewhere in this volume.

The external relationships of the library also require careful administration in an automated environment. Among the more critical are those between the library and off-campus suppliers of books and serials, of equipment and software, and of bibliographic and other data files, as well as between the library and the on-campus computing organizations. This article focuses on the nature, content and organization of one set of these external relationships, that between the library and the campus computing centers. The first section below reviews some of the general types of organizational structure in which to conceptualize and administer these relationships; the second section then provides a framework for conceiving of and administering the specific work relationships between the two organizations.

STRUCTURAL RELATIONSHIPS BETWEEN LIBRARY AND COMPUTING ORGANIZATIONS

Estrangement

During the 1960s and 1970s, after brief and tentative periods of joint activity, libraries and campus computer centers drifted apart.

The computer centers focused on critical administrative services, such as automated accounting systems, and generally were sole providers of academic computing resources. Libraries needed general administrative services, but also demanded what seemed, in the abstract, to be an inventory control system, much like other administrative control systems being developed within the computer centers. However, bibliographic data structures proved so unlike the type of structures being developed for the campus administrative systems that libraries typically gained little advantage from cooperation with the computer center. Instead, the library world developed a standard format for machine-readable cataloging (MARC). Some libraries struck out entirely on their own, while others joined together and pooled their resources to develop computer systems principally for cataloging and acquisitions in national and regional services like OCLC, UTLAS, WLN and, later, RLIN.[2] The distance between libraries and computer centers widened and the gap seemed, at times, virtually impassable. For example, in 1974, one observer argued that the major factors inhibiting the application of computers to the library included "(A) Governance, organization and management of the computer facility; (B) Personnel in the computer facility; and (C) Deficiencies in the library environment." For closer and more effective relationships between the two organizations, "substantial future change" would be required.[3]

During the 1980s, the economics of computing did change dramatically. As processors shrunk in size and increased in power, costs plunged. Individual campus departments invested in their own minicomputer systems and faculty and students moved in droves to purchase personal computer systems. The perceptions—no doubt accurate on many campuses—that the computing centers could not adequately meet the new and growing demands for computing and that they served more to hinder than to facilitate automation efforts tended to justify the distribution of computers and computing away from computer "centers." The need for central computing, particularly for administrative services, did not disappear, but the new mix of centralized and distributed computing presented the need for new kinds of centralized services. Central computing organizations responded, some more effectively and quickly than others, with efforts designed to leverage central computing, coordinate distributed computing activities and connect the central and distributed users through campus networks. The challenge and scope of these new responsibilities led many colleges and universities to establish a new high level administrative position, often known colloquially as the campus computer "czar."[4]

Meanwhile, as academic computing generally moved away from the computer center, the changing economics of the last decade had the peculiar and ironic effect in many cases of driving library computing back to campus where it has become a critical concern of the central campus computing organizations. The drop in the costs of computers and computing meant that libraries could now afford, or more easily afford, to obtain and manage their own equipment on which they could mount their own databases and control systems. The new affordability of the technology opened a market to which vendors responded with commercial systems, many of which combined hardware and software, and which were designed specifically for the various bibliographic control needs of libraries. In some cases, online circulation systems and public access catalogs supplemented the automated cataloging and acquisition functions provided by the national and regional utilities; in other cases, local acquisitions and cataloging systems supplanted some or all of the services of the utilities.

Libraries, which usually rank among the largest departments on campus, looked then to house these computer-based systems on campus. Some libraries managed to remain independent of the campus computing organization and to build and maintain within the library a computing facility for their own databases and control systems. But they did so at the same time as central computing organizations began articulating a newly identified responsibility for economizing and coordinating departmental computing systems and for distributing critical, widely-used electronic information resources, like the library's catalog, via campus computer networks.

Although tension still remains and, in some cases, the two organizations may have very little to do with one another, the distance between libraries and computer centers has generally narrowed over the last decade. The two organizations have come increasingly to recognize, at the broadest level, their mutual interest in delivering electronic information to the academic community. The convergence of interest has opened a variety of opportunities for structurally reorganizing campus information systems. In general and in addition to the mode of estrangement, two types of reorganized structures have emerged. The first posits a new, single, merged organization in place of the library and the computer center. The second assumes the structural integrity of the two organizations, but posits a set of partnership relations between them.

Mergers and Takeovers

One obvious way of administering the mutual interest between computer centers and libraries is simply to merge the two organizations. This structural option has received much attention in recent years, particularly in the library literature, as merged library/computing organizations have actually developed on some campuses. Consolidated organizations have appeared under the library director (the so-called "Columbia" model), under the director of computing (the "Carnegie-Mellon" model) and under some form of shared leadership (the "Stanford" model).[5]

The argument for consolidation typically emphasizes the complementary strengths of the two organizations in pursuit of the common goal of delivering electronic information. The important qualities of the computer center that are often emphasized include presumed 24 hour access, unlimited and cost effective storage systems, direct access to local and remote data sources, easily manipulable files and technical expertise. The balancing qualities stressed on behalf of the library include a strong service orientation, highly structured files and collections, common modes of access which diminish the need for extensive user training, generally free access, and subject expertise.[6]

According to Patricia Battin, in a concise statement of the argument for organizational merger, "the integration of libraries and computer centers, each with its specific strengths and expertise, will provide one-stop shopping for the university community and a stabilizing planning mechanism for effective and flexible response to rapidly changing technologies."[7] Others have recognized the difficulties of achieving a successful merger but have assumed nevertheless that the natural outcome of interaction between libraries and computer centers will be "a true union of interests and functions."[8]

And one observer has drawn an elaborate and vivid biological metaphor, hinging on concepts of entropy, evolution, and extinction, to suggest that even if the two organizations do not formally merge, they will likely grow to resemble one another until they are virtually indistinguishable.[9]

Partnerships

Of course, an organizational merger is not the only path that leads to the realization of mutual interest between libraries and computer centers. Indeed, the very features — technical versus subject expertise, for example — that appear to be complementary and to lead to mergers in some universities may well in others reflect vastly different personalities, cultural orientations, political alliances, and organizational histories. Underlying personal, cultural, political and organizational differences greatly complicate the relationships between libraries and computing centers and, where they exist, these various differences actively militate against merged organizations.[10]

Recent studies indicate that very few institutions are known to be contemplating a merger of the library and computer center, and even fewer have actually tried to accomplish it.[11] As Richard Dougherty has argued, differences between libraries and computer centers are "so great from an organizational viewpoint" that administrative models that depend on the concept of consolidating the two units into one are unlikely to predominate in the near term.[12] Alternative administrative structures are necessary that accommodate the differences between the organizations, recognize the separate structural integrity of each unit and yet foster the effective pursuit of common goals. Such structures of cooperation and collaboration are common and typically fall under the general rubric of partnership.

The notion of a partnership refers in general to a "working relationship between two units that are interdependent or in which one relies on another for service."[13] In a strict, or legal, sense, partnerships are founded on formal agreements which specify the rights and obligations of each party. But the working relationship may also be much less formal, involving exchanges of information, services, tools and other resources on a regular, *ad hoc*, or even open-ended basis.

The purposes and forms of the partnerships that are presently emerging between libraries and campus computing organizations are many and varied. Service agreements, under which the computer center operates the computer facility for the library system, is one type, for example, and they may take the form of written contracts or letters of understanding, or they may be implemented simply under periodic planning and operations meetings between the library and computer center staff. The purposes of partnership ultimately reflect the kinds and nature of the interdependencies between the organizations, and the formality of the relationships depends, in part, on the nature of the personalities involved and the larger political and historical climate on campus in which the organizations operate. In any case, whatever specific purposes they serve and whatever form they take, the emerging partnerships form the foundations of a division of labor that will shape (or hinder) the development of future campus information services. Proper administration of the relationships thus is critical and requires a systematic framework from which to view the common work in which libraries and computing organizations currently engage one another. The following section is intended to help articulate such a framework.

WORKING RELATIONSHIPS BETWEEN LIBRARY AND COMPUTING ORGANIZATIONS

Structural relationships between libraries and campus computing organizations range between the extremes of estrangement and coalescence, and occupy a large middle ground of emerging interdependence, cooperation and collaboration. For purposes of analyzing, appreciating and administering the working relationships in the middle ground—the extremes need to be managed too, of course, but each in ways that are different and beyond the scope of this paper to explicate—it is useful to distinguish three components of the working relationships. First, one has to ask about the overall direction that the joint application of effort, equipment and tools is taking. Is it a strategic application for one or both organizations, or is it entrepreneurial in nature? Strategic applications are those that aim significantly to advance the mission of the business unit, in this case the library or the computer center. Entrepreneurial applications are so called because, though their impact on the goals is less certain, they promise to open new lines of business, cut costs of existing services, or improve the quality of their delivery. They are less directly tied to stated business goals, and are more experimental in nature.

Second, given the overall direction of the application of work, it is useful to distinguish the type of work by function. Is the work programmatic or administrative in nature? Programmatic, or "line," functions directly advance the mission of the organization; administrative functions serve to set directions and to provide operational support for programmatic or line functions.[14]

Third, within this general goal-oriented framework, which highlights the overall organizational missions and the functions that lead to them, one can then distinguish the specific task arenas that are the subject of organizational partnerships and collaboration. Here, three arenas are explored: the library's local system, the electronic administration of the library and the so-called "electronic campus," which is treated generally as an entrepreneurial category with implications for both programmatic and administrative functions (see Figure 1).[15] In each of these arenas, different interests of libraries and campus computing organizations intersect.

The Library's Local System

The general missions and goals of college and research libraries and their strategies for the use of computer technology vary considerably in articulateness and conviction of expression, and in empha-

Application	Strategic		Entrepreneurial	
Function	Programmatic	Administrative	Programmatic	Administrative
Task Arenas	Local System	Electronic Administration	Electronic Campus	

Figure 1

sis and priority depending on such factors as size, resources available, and degree of automation. However, for purposes of this discussion, most of the larger college and research libraries are assumed to share, as a central programmatic function, a critical interest in the development of what is commonly known as the "local system." The concept of a "local system" generally refers to the set of automated tools available on campus for library operations and is opposed to those that are available as part of the "distant" system in which they may participate as part of a regional or national bibliographic entity. The category of "library operations" includes most of the traditional library functions: collection development, technical services (acquisitions, cataloging, serials control, labelling and plating, preservation) and public services (circulation, interlibrary loan, public access).

Despite frequent predictions about imminent changes in the structure and function of libraries, key local system activity will, for the foreseeable future, be concentrated largely on providing an ordered and integrated set of automated tools for the traditional library services. The principal areas of activity will likely include the following: development of the quality and integrity of the local database through the development of local automated maintenance and authority control processes; accelerated growth of the local database through local automated retrospective conversion processes; enhancement of local cataloging and collection development processes through the addition and maintenance of locally mounted resource files and through improved access to national bibliographic utilities; automation of acquisition functions through electronic interaction with vendors and with college and university accounting and fiscal control entities; addition and enhancement of support for non-roman scripts; improvement and standardization of the user interface to the public catalog; extension of access to the public catalog via campus networks; and use of local automated resources to improve document delivery. Again, emphases and priorities undoubtedly vary from library to library, but these categories probably cover the most critical areas of activity.

In this laundry list of tasks, there is ample room for computer center—library cooperation. However, underlying and facilitating all the activities is the central set of tools, the computer hardware and software, that comprises the library's automated system. And it is in the selection, acquisition, installation and operation of the computer facilities themselves that the campus computing organizations typically have the most to offer the library.

In some cases, computer center staff have expertise needed to assist librarians in their analyses of systems requirements and in their evaluation and selection of hardware and software options. Because the purchase of the requisite hardware and software typically requires a significant expense, the computing organization more frequently is able to afford the library both substantial experience in dealing with vendors and a position of relative strength in negotiations. Often, the computer center can also leverage existing hardware and software components. By allowing the library to share the use of these components and by setting usage prices at the margin, it can save the library, and the institution as a whole, substantial sums against the purchase of new or standalone equipment. And even if it participates in none of these preliminary activities, the computer center almost always can offer sufficient economies of scale in space, operations services and/or programming expertise for the library to invite its participation in the installation and operation of the local system.

To the extent that the computer center does participate in the operation of the library's local system, the division of labor between the two organizations may vary. Typical modes of interaction, however, find the library covering the maintenance costs of any hardware it buys, providing paper, magnetic tapes and other supplies, owning and maintaining the database and the application software, as well as training system users and providing a liaison between the user and the computer center. For its part, the computer center responsibilities include maintenance of the underlying hardware and software environment, capacity and performance monitoring and planning, design and maintenance of procedures for the successful operation of the online and batch features of the system, maintenance of terminal and workstation communications links, backups and disaster recovery, security administration, and troubleshooting.[16]

In this model, the library is the client and the computer center is the service provider. Funding and specific terms of the relationship vary from institution to institution and, as in any client/provider relationship, so does the tension, both productive and conflictive. But the strength of the mutual interest in the library's local system can significantly affect the tension, and the processes by which it is addressed in the two organizations. The local system is of strategic programmatic interest in the library; it is its life-blood. In cases where the online catalog becomes a visible and valuable deliverable on the campus network, when it becomes the life-blood also of the computing organization, then the client/provider roles are reversed, the relationship between the two organizations balance, and a true partnership in mutual interest may emerge. And, if it is not sufficiently prepared, the library, now a provider of a database to its client, the computer center, may find its internal priorities shifting radically.

As the library's product, its electronic database, moves on the campus network in open competition with other electronic information sources, scholarly demand for features and services may well require fundamental and, perhaps, unexpected changes in the library's products and services, and in the organization designed to deliver them. Automation of technical services departments has led, for example, to increased use of copy and minimum-level cataloging. Combined with growing reader demand for access services, such as the ability to transfer bibliographic information from the library's online catalog to a scholar's personal database, automation of the local system may ultimately lead to a variety of innovative and unanticipated ways both of conceptualizing the traditional distinctions between technical and public services, and of organizing and allocating resources within and between the two departments.[17]

Electronic Administration

The library's "local system" is closely related to, but is usefully distinguished, both from the set of automated tools available within the library for electronic administration and from the tools available to the library as members of what might be termed the "electronic campus." So-called electronic administration within the library includes the use of large subsystems such as the university's accounting system and various personnel tracking systems. It also includes subsystems for workgroup communication and management, such as electronic mail connections, decision-support systems that may involve spreadsheets or database management systems on personal computers, and document production on PC-based systems. Because computer-based subsystems that serve library administration are typically part of larger systems that the computer center delivers to the wider campus community, support within academic libraries of the use of institution-wide accounting and personnel systems and of microcomputing is typically and consciously designed not to supplant, but to build on and extend the central services of the computing organizations.

Electronic administration is often overlooked as a critical arena of interdependent activity between the library and the campus computing organization. But here the mutual interest of the organizations in automation is particularly strong. Provision of the electronic tools and information that serve to enhance the quality of management across campus — delivery of so-called management information systems — is almost always a strategic program goal for the computer center. For the library, use of such systems is also a strategic goal, but not a programmatic one. Rather, electronic administration within the library is one set of tools for rationally and efficiently determining the direction, weighing the priorities and providing documentary and informational support for the delivery of the set of programs, like the development of the local system, that serve strategically to define and achieve the library's central missions.

These complementary interests of the computer center and the library in electronic administration provide fertile grounds for the growth of effective and strategic forms of partnership between the two organizations. Library and computer center staff can, for example, work together to integrate the library's automated acquisition system, in which invoices are logged and payments authorized, with the university's automated disbursements and accounting systems, from which payments for library materials are made and accounted. Such a cooperative effort can substantially improve the management of the library's collection development programs and can make the entire institutional information system more timely, comprehensive and accurate as a general university management tool. But the seeds of cooperation between the two organizations in the arena of electronic administration are often buried in the subtleties of a decentralized university structure, and nowhere is this more evident than in the administrative applications of microcomputers.

In most colleges and universities, administrative use of microcomputers is organized both within the central computing facilities and in the various departments, of which the library is usually among the largest. In some cases, the central computer facility will have the authority to mandate the types of hardware and software that a department may purchase and use. For the most part, however, the budgetary authority to purchase microcomputers for administrative use typically resides in university departments. Thus, in the absence of a central mandate, the fundamental principle of microcomputer organization is that decisions about what kinds of hardware and software to purchase and how to use and support them are made at the departmental level, not centrally. Even in such cases, however, the central computing facilities do aim to influence and coordinate decisions made in the departments, and their success is determined, in part, by the nature of the central organization for microcomputer support and, in greater part, by the ways that the organization joins with the departments, such as the library, as partners in the support enterprise.

The strategic goals for microcomputer support at the central level are to identify reliable vendors and cost effective products, to achieve economies of scale within the university for the support and use of the microcomputer products that departments have purchased, and in other ways to assist and enfranchise microcomputer users on campus. The primary organization on campus to identify reliable microcomputer vendors and cost effective products is typically a microcomputer store that the computer center either has created as an internal business unit or sponsors as an external unit. The store negotiates substantial volume discounts and then buys, resells and supports hardware and some software products. Either the same unit or a separate one also negotiates volume or educational discounts — and site licenses where possible — and then buys and resells a limited selection of software for the supported hardware. For products not provided by either of these two organizations, departments can seek the assistance of the university purchasing department or deal directly with commercial vendors.

The discounts and purchasing services available at the microcomputer store of the computer center provide substantial incentives for university departments, as well as individual faculty and students, effectively to channel their purchases of hardware and software to a standard, and relatively narrow, set of vendors and products. Given these incentives, microcomputer purchases generally create on campus a critical mass of individuals who are using the same standard set of equipment and speaking essentially the same electronic languages.[18] In support of this user population and to advance the office automation strategies they represent, a variety of central groups have newly emerged or have adapted existing services: groups of technicians to provide microcomputer hardware maintenance; systems programming groups to develop useful tools primarily for microcomputer communication and networking; applications groups to offer fee-for-service programming; and user services groups to train, consult, write documentation, and organize user groups.

Despite the substantial alignments of central resources to support campus microcomputing, the central computing facilities generally do not have the resources to concentrate in detail on the day-to-day issues of direct user support. Those staff in the library then who need help assessing their microcomputer needs, specifying, purchasing and installing equipment, recovering a lost file from their hard disk, using their word processor and printer to prepare a proposal for a new program of bibliographic instruction, or setting up a spreadsheet to collect statistics on cataloging output must often help themselves or turn to one another for assistance. It is, of course, in the library's interest to organize and manage staff expertise — or the lack of it — to insure that individuals are or become smart enough to make effective use of the investment in electronic administration. In many larger libraries, one common organizational technique is to dedicate at least one staff position, wholly or partly, to develop microcomputer expertise and to provide needed support.

Although the support efforts of the central computing organization are focused more on the overall microcomputing environment on campus, a variety of creative ventures between library and computer center have emerged to cement the broad channels of support that the computer center has carved and to leverage and provide added value to the daily support efforts within the library. For example, the computer center may invite library staff to join a variety of key boards and committees that create central computing policy and procedures. By participating with computer center staff in groups that help determine the course of the campus network, the kinds of equipment and software supplied in the campus store, the procedures for equipment and software purchases, or the kinds of database products that will be supported, library staff are exposed to the range of central services they can draw on to enhance the library's use of microcomputers and they can insure that the library's interests are broadly and specifically represented in the computer center.

Another type of creative venture between the library and the computer center in this arena is for the computer center to offer the library certain kinds of preferential treatment. In exchange for such treatment, the library would shoulder certain support duties that would otherwise be the responsibility of the central organization. For example, the hardware maintenance group may reduce service charges for or assign a higher priority to library service calls if library staff perform an initial set of diagnostic steps that precisely and accurately determine the nature of the problem. The exercise of library expertise saves the central staff from the difficult and time-consuming tasks of problem determination and enables them simply and quickly to take the appropriate corrective measures.

The successful partnerships that emerge from these various relationships redound to the library in the form of more effective internal administrative support. The library has the opportunity to assert a campus-wide leadership position in the day-to-day operation of a microcomputer-based electronic administration, and the computer center can point to the library as an exemplar in its model of computer support in a decentralized organization. Moreover, the subtle alliances that these relationships build around both the library's and the university's increasingly microcomputer-based electronic administration have the added, synergistic effect of building a computer center/library team that is better capable of supporting the academic use of microcomputing.[19] The range and tone of harmony between the library and the computer center in the administrative arena thus may reverberate deeply.

The Electronic Campus

The electronic campus as a vision of the college or university of the future has an enormous appeal—at least in the abstract. The concept, however, is presently an amorphous, ill-defined one, enveloped in uncertainty. To be sure, there are strategic pockets—for example, the library's local system and its electronic administration—where critical components of campus automation are relatively well-defined and the rates of growth and development are subject to reasonable fiscal and administrative controls. But, in general, the number of computer-based tools available on campus is growing rapidly, their application to university programs and administration is largely unproven, if they have been tested at all, and the rate at which the technology itself is changing is sometimes staggering. As a result, today's electronic campus remains largely the province of entrepreneurs, those risk-taking institutions, notably Carnegie-Mellon University and the Massachusetts Institute of Technology, and segments of other institutions willing to invest in and develop uncertain and unproven technology.

Because one assumes that computer-based technologies will eventually facilitate, or enable, campus automation, even if the specific applications are presently not well-understood, the tools on today's electronic campus are known as "enabling technologies." They fall generally into four classes: imaging, database management, networking, and artificial intelligence/expert systems.[20] How and whether the technology in these various categories will affect the future of academic libraries is a subject of much interest, and the answer on each campus will depend in part on how and whether the local computing organization sees fit itself to invest in the technology. The nature and shape of the electronic campus thus depends on the ways in which the library and computer center collaborate—or fail to—in these various technology arenas.

The first category of tools emerging on the electronic campus include those that enable the production, storage, retrieval and use of digital images. The most important challenges for the library and the computer center are to distinguish the various applications of image technology and provide appropriate leadership in each area. Expertise is required in image processing to convert existing data — collections of manuscripts and archives, film, maps, artifacts, and possibly even the library's card catalog — for preservation and general use in electronic forms. Digital images also are proliferating directly as a result of computer algorithms and operations: CAD-CAM drawings in engineering, architectural plans, choreographies and cartoons. Finally, and perhaps most difficult to handle in terms of storage and classification, is the need to file and access the vast amounts of digital images being generated in the automatic observation of natural processes — images of bio-medical processes, for example, and those generated by earth satellites and space probes.[21]

The second emergent set of tools relates to database management. Any systematic attention on campus to image-based data will quickly outstrip conventional forms of storage; an investment in optical storage devices may eventually help relieve these pressures. Meanwhile, character-based sources of textual, bibliographic and numeric data are proliferating on and off-campus. Some of these sources are becoming and will continue to become accessible through the interface to the library database; others are and will be managed in various other ways. In any case, libraries and computer centers will have to find and implement technical solutions to link together as appropriate the various databases that are distributed across different media, under the control of different computers and organized under different data structures. For example, will a user be able to know, simply from searching an article-level database on one machine, whether the library holdings database, which is stored in a different computer across campus, contains a record of the journal in which a desired article appears?

The third category of tools — communications networks — provides the basis upon which the structured paths among distributed databases may be built for intersystem searching and access, and the choices here may seem bewildering. The computing organization, the library, and other departments as well, have to cooperate to select media and data link and transport level protocols for both the campus backbone network and departmental-level local area networks. In a world of multiple standards, mechanisms to facilitate transfer of data traffic from one set of standard protocols to another, both on and off campus must also be provided. Means to secure the data traversing the network from being corrupted, lost or stolen are critical, and all of this is not to mention whether, given all other network requirements, the linked system protocols currently being developed and implemented are sufficiently general to facilitate not only intersystem searching and retrieval but also direct linkages between data structures of different types.

Artificial intelligence and expert system tools comprise the fourth category of emergent information tools on today's electronic campus. Computer center and library cooperation will almost certainly be necessary in this arena to economize on the relatively specialized and expensive hardware and software needed for artificial intelligence applications, and to resolve at an institutional level questions of intellectual property and publication rights that arise in the construction of electronic knowledge bases. Meanwhile, librarians and technical staff may work together in specific and narrowly circumscribed research and discipline domains where financial and legal issues have less effect. Librarians can specifically contribute to the engineering of knowledge bases in these areas by assisting in the informatic work, that is accumulating necessary information in structured forms. They will also undoubtedly continue to pursue the applicability of expert systems to such internal processing domains of the library as cataloging and reference. In the longer term, one can expect the appearance of substantial expert systems for general access within the scholarly community, and eventually the appearance of multiple, integrated systems. Both the library and the computer center will need to cooperate both in the construction of these systems and in providing general, affordable access.[22]

Because the electronic campus in each of these four areas is subject today to such flux and to standards that are moving targets if they exist at all, few libraries and computing organizations are yet willing, either together or separately, to commit to long term strategies. Furthermore, in most institutions, these organizations have only just begun to engage in the tough political processes necessary to hammer out a reasonable set of strategy options from which to choose and assign responsibilities over the long haul. Nevertheless, an ongoing strategic planning process is an absolutely essential ingredient, and probably one of the cheapest components, in the long-term process of incorporating high-risk, entrepreneur-driven technologies from the electronic campus into the standard programs and administration of library and other academic departments. The planning process should include the library, the computing organization and other constituent groups on campus and should aim systematically to evaluate the tools and technologies on the electronic campus for their possible application to the goals and missions of each department and the wider institution.

Within the framework of a longer range planning process, the library and the computer center may, in cooperation, decide to make specific investments in promising, but relatively unstable, technologies under the rubric of a formal feasibility study or a pilot project. Many libraries and computing centers are already exploring, experimenting with and adopting short term networking strategies and are actively trying to identify and respond to the service implications of radically decentralized computing and of the generation and proliferation of new forms of graphic and textual information and retrieval mechanisms. But as fiscal pressures build within colleges and universities, the demand for an even more aggressive stance to the new technologies will undoubtedly grow. Not only will it be necessary for libraries and computer centers to deploy new technologies to improve the quality and quantity of products and services in the academic business, it will also be crucial for them to lead the institution in resisting the continuing temptation to apply a technological fix to problems or processes that can or should be addressed in other more natural, economical or creative ways. If the experience needed to know when to turn to the electronic campus and when not to do so cannot be gained directly through selected feasibility studies and pilot programs, then the library and computer center must at least adopt a strong posture of closely tracking those organizations and institutions that are able directly to invest in new technology.

SUMMARY

In the context of an emerging electronic campus, where the assertion that "we have a computer" thoroughly applies, some observers have suggested that the meaning of "library" will surely change. It may. But to date, there is more agreement that a change will occur than there is consensus about the nature or possible effects of that change.

By its very nature, the computer and the information technology that it represents implies a social organization that is so richly complex in interdependence and interaction that the consequences of computer-based automation seem to defy prediction and to hold enormous risk. The administration of computer-based automation, therefore, must be governed by conceptual models that explicitly incorporate notions of complex social organization and interdependence. This paper has emphasized one set of complex and interdependent relationships associated with computer-based automation in libraries: the relationships between the library and the campus computing organization. For purposes of identifying key administrative issues, it has then distinguished various structural relationships between the two organizations—whether they are estranged, merged or in partnership. Focusing on partnership relationships, the paper then has argued that variation in the types of work performed within the partnership—whether it is strategic or entrepreneurial in application and programmatic or administrative in function—help determine whether the claim that "we have a computer" in an automated library is a statement of success, or dismal failure.

NOTES

1. Arno Penzias, *Ideas and Information: Managing in a High-Tech World* (New York: W.W. Norton & Company, 1989).

2. See Caroline Arms, "Libraries and Electronic Information: The Technological Context, Part One," *EDUCOM Review* 24 (Summer, 1989): 38-43.

3. Allen B. Veaner, "Institutional Political and Fiscal Factors in the Development of Library Automation, 1967-71," *Journal of Library Automation* 7 (March, 1974): 5-25.

4. See Anne Woodsworth, "Libraries and the Chief Information Officer: Implications and Trends," *Library Hi Tech* 21 (March, 1988): 37-44.

5. David C. Weber, "University Libraries and Campus Information Technology Organizations: Who Is in Charge Here?" *Journal of Library Administration* 9, no. 4 (1988): 5-19.

6. Pat Molholt, "On Converging Paths: the Computing Center and the Library," *Journal of Academic Librarianship* 11 (November, 1985): 284-88.

7. Patricia Battin, "The Electronic Library—A Vision for the Future," *EDUCOM Bulletin* 19 (Summer, 1984): 12-17, 34.

8. Diane J. Cimbala, "The Scholarly Information Center: An Organizational Model," *College and Research Libraries* 48 (September, 1987): 393-398.

9. Timothy C. Weiskel, "Libraries as Life Systems: Information, Entropy and Coevolution on Campus," *College and Research Libraries* 47 (November, 1986): 545-563. For an earlier version of the argument discussed in this paragraph, see Helen Howard, "Innovation in University Organization: The Communication Model," *Journal of Academic Librarianship* 6 (May, 1980): 77-82.

10. See Cimbala, "The Scholarly Information Center;" John R. Sack, "Open Systems for Open Minds: Building the Library without Walls," *College and Research Libraries* 47 (November, 1986): 535-544; and David R. MacDonald, "The Ingredients of a Good Relationship: The Library's Point of View," *Libraries & Computing Centers* 6 (January, 1988): 1-2.

11. Woodsworth, "Libraries and the Chief Information Officer."

12. Richard M. Dougherty, "Libraries and Computing Centers: A Blueprint for Collaboration," *College and Research Libraries* 48 (July, 1987): 289-296. See also Susan K. Martin, "Library Management and Emerging Technology: The Immovable Force and the Irresistible Object," *Library Trends* 37, no. 3 (1989): 374-382.

13. Anne Woodsworth and James F. Williams II, "Computing Centers and Libraries: In Passage Toward Partnerships," *Library Administration & Management* 2 (March, 1988): 85-90.

14. For these distinctions, I have drawn on a report that I and my colleague, Robert W. Boyd, authored for the Yale University Library Microcomputer Advisory Board, entitled "Library Microcomputer Products Selection and Support Guidelines," 1989.

15. For a related use of these distinctions, see Lynne Personius, Jerry Persons, and Donald Waters, "Local Systems and the Research Libraries Group: Some Considerations for a Long-Range Technical Plan," Local Systems Planning Committee, Research Libraries Group, March 26, 1989.

16. Woodsworth and Williams, "Computing Centers and Libraries."

17. See, for example, Judith Herschman et al., "Tampering with the Online Catalog: A Look at the Issues—A Symposium," *Journal of Academic Librarianship* 12, no. 6 (1987): 340-349; Marie Bednar, "Automation of Cataloging: Effects on Use of Staff, Efficiency, and Service to Patrons," *Journal of Academic Librarianship* 14, no. 3 (1988): 145-149; and Timothy C. Weiskel, "University Libraries, Integrated Scholarly Information Systems (ISIS), and the Changing Character of Academic Research," *Library Hi Tech* 6, no. 4 (1988): 7-28.

18. Robert W. Boyd, "Microcomputer Product Standards," *Systems Office Communique #5* (New Haven: Yale University Library, 1989).

19. As is now well known, both the library and the computer center have much at stake both separately and together in support of microcomputing for academic purposes. Few academic libraries today are without at least one microcomputer that provides readers access to a CD-ROM database product. Similarly,

most academic computing organizations maintain one or more clusters of micro-computers for faculty and students to use publicly in support of classroom or research work. And together, the organizations often cooperate in detailed ways. The library may provide space for the microcomputer cluster, as well as collect, catalog and circulate the inventory of software, while the computer center may supply and maintain the machines, pay for some or all of the software and provide the user support staff.

Among much else on the academic use of microcomputers on campus and in libraries, see Susan S. Lukesh, "Microcomputer Use in Higher Education: Summary of a Survey," *Educom Bulletin* (Fall, 1987): 13-17; Howard Curtis, ed., *Public Access Microcomputers in Academic Libraries: the Mann Library Model at Cornell University*, (Chicago: American Library Association, 1987); Association of Research Libraries, Office of Management Studies, *Microcomputer Software Policies in ARL Libraries, Kit 123* (Washington, D.C.: Association of Research Libraries, April 1986); Jim Milliot, *Micros at Work: Case Studies of Microcomputers in Libraries* (White Plains, N.Y.: Knowledge Industry Publications, 1985); and Jeannine Uppgard, ed., *Developing Microcomputer Work Areas in Academic Libraries* (Westport, CT: Meckler Corporation, 1988).

20. Lawrence E. Murr and James B. Williams, "The Roles of the Future Library," *Library Hi Tech*, 5 (Fall, 1987): 7-23.

21. Robert M. Hayes, "Concluding Address," in *Proceedings of the Conference on Application of Scanning Methodologies in Libraries* (Beltsville, MD: National Agricultural Library, 1988), pp. 133-140.

22. Murr and Williams, "The Roles of the Future Library." See also Linda C. Smith, "Artificial Intelligence and Information Retrieval," in Martha E. Williams, ed., *Annual Review of Information Science and Technology*, 22 (Amsterdam: Elsevier Science Publishers, 1987), pp. 41-77; and John Richardson, Jr., "Toward an Expert System for Reference Service: A Research Agenda for the 1990s," *College and Research Libraries*, 50 (March, 1989): 231-248.

Automation and the Renaissance Technical Services Librarian

Elizabeth Dickinson Nichols

Any technical services manager who has ever been involved in planning and implementing an automated system feels like a mother who has just given birth. We tend to treat automating like a new and unique undertaking that no one else has ever experienced in quite the same way before. It has its moments of joy and great achievement. It also inevitably has an element of pain.

Giving birth to an automated system can be stressful and thankless when there is little support in the process, but it can also bring the work "family" closer together with the proper preparation. Out of the process, if managed well, will be born a new, more cohesive and flexible staff. Job duties will change, and so will the skill requirements of individual staff members.

THE LITERATURE

Perhaps because we tend to treat each automation project as a unique birthing experience there is little in the literature on the human side of automating other than case studies and personal accounts. Hill summarizes a number of experiences and speculates on automation's impact by 1995.[1] Rooks and Thompson also note the paucity of literature on the human side of automation and make some observations from their own experience on the questions that will occur most often to staff who are in the throes of automation.[2] Several useful articles for those wishing to maximize the beneficial

Elizabeth Dickinson Nichols is Division Manager, Technical Services, Stockton-San Joaquin County Public Library, CA.

human impact and minimize the problems of automating are contained in the proceedings of the 1985 Clinic on Library Applications of Data Processing at the University of Illinois at Urbana-Champaign.[3]

One of the few original research reports in the area of automation's impact on technical services organizational structure was conducted by the Association for Research Libraries.[4] ARL libraries were polled in the fall of 1984 to determine whether there had been any automation-induced reorganization of technical services.

Few authors have concentrated on automation's human and organizational impact within public libraries and little can be considered original research. Freedman's lengthy experience with public library automation is recounted in "Automation and the Future of Technical Services," along with a prognosis for how technical services may further change as a result of computerization.[5] The experiences of Pikes Peak Library District are well documented in several publications, in particular, Dowlin's *Electronic Library.*[6] Nichols offers advice for improving automation's acceptance by staff and public.[7] Bishoff concentrates upon how automation has impacted the need for catalogers in public libraries.[8] Nichin reports increased professionalism and, in addition, pay raises, associated with technical services automation.[9]

An analysis of the published record reveals that, while there is little consensus on the organizational impact of automation on technical services, many similarities exist in the experiences of libraries with other human factors. Perhaps the automation birthing process is not so unique after all!

While this article is intended to focus primarily as a guide to public libraries in the process of automating, much will be equally applicable to all types and sizes of libraries. Humans react to change in similar ways no matter what the setting. There are standard, well tested ways of handling the change process.

As a matter of definition, for the purposes of this article the areas considered to be within technical services are acquisitions, cataloging, materials processing, circulation services, and automated systems management. These are the materials handling, system-wide support services that maintain catalog and/or patron files in a typical integrated library system.

AUTOMATION'S GENERAL HUMAN IMPACT

It seems human nature to resist change. Automation brings in its wake massive change and, in many cases, resistance. Is this because we are naturally lazy? Would we rather work on tried and true routines to better afford the time to daydream about our next vacation? While for some library workers change may thwart personal aims, for most there are more worthy reasons for anxiety.

Risk-Avoidance: Librarians tend to be risk-avoiders, not risk-seekers. We fear the consequences of being wrong—the loss of productivity, waste of scarce library resources, loss of public and political support, as well as loss of personal face and status. Automation is a particularly high risk area. Library system suppliers go bankrupt. They are sometimes bought out by others with less zealous interest in bettering library clientele. They almost inevitably deliver less than was called for under contract, or are late on producing some system functions. Library automation comes across like a mine field to the risk-avoider.

Productivity Loss: Library workers are generally productivity conscious. No cataloger, for example, likes to see new materials backlog while a retrospective conversion project is being completed. Planning and implementing an automated library system takes an extraordinary amount of time to complete. This process impacts on the entire staff. Productivity losses created during the automation start-up period will produce stress as ongoing work piles up. Further, the training process for an automated system will add up to as much as 50% of the cost of an entire automation project, 20% during the first year, and 30% over subsequent years.[10] This translates into ongoing large amounts of staff time that must be devoted to an automated system at the expense of ongoing workload. Industrial studies have shown that loss of productivity can significantly increase absenteeism, turnover, and worker resistance to change.[11]

Service Interruptions: Planning and implementing an automated system may also lead to service interruptions and glitches which are more noticeable to the public than are the delays that occur in a manual environment. The public rarely knows when a backlog in catalog card filing leads to diminished access to the library's collection. In the manually run library if something goes wrong it generally impacts just one branch library or department. When the computer goes down everyone knows it. When notices fail to print from the automated request system, lots of calls are received from complaining patrons. When an aging, over-extended automated system slows down it causes longer lines at every check-out point. The over-extended older system may also require catalogers and acquisitions staff to limit the periods during the day when they may have access to resource-intensive subsystems. Again, the stress level is magnified and extended to virtually all staff and a large segment of users when the library system is automated.

Cog in the Wheel: Non-automated library work units are organized around independent files. For catalogers the main manual file is the paper shelflist. For acquisitions staff the order file provides the central focus. Usually each non-automated branch library has its own card catalog of that library's specific holdings. Automation has a centralizing effect by consolidating files into one integrated system available to all, but, in most libraries, managed centrally. In order to effectively automate virtually all policies and procedures had to be analyzed and merged into standardized, system-wide dictums. The consequence has meant a loss of control by individual line supervisors and staff members of many procedures. Application of policy and procedure is less subject to interpretation when they are controlled by a parameterized computer program and specific computer routines. Staff often cannot even vary the order in which tasks are preformed without negative consequences to online routines. This degree of control can rub against the grain. Librarians are most highly motivated by "challenging and varied work" and need latitude in decision-making.[12] The prospect of robot-like adherence to computers can lead to lowered job satisfaction and lowered sense of professionalism.[13]

Craig Brod terms many of the negative impacts of automation "technostress."[14] He catalogs many of the symptoms including:

- Magnification of mistakes leading to pressure-cooker conditions to fix.
- Work overload because of the tendency for supervisors to quantify productivity.

- Increased physical complaints such as eye- and back-strain, carpal-tunnel syndrome, headaches, fatigue.
- Inability to stand interruption while working at the computer. The machine mesmerizes.
- Limited job creativity because the machine dictates process. There is a tendency to concentrate on the work at hand and not to "blue sky" possible creative solutions.
- Distortion of time.
- Stress due to limited control over the job. Work is monitored and standardized.
- Computerization fosters specialization because the job complexity brought on with automation demands technical know-how rather than "renaissance" generalist background. Brod contends this makes it harder to move from job to job.
- Greater worker isolation as individuals are chained to their computers.[15]

Most library technical services managers who have participated in the automation of library procedures will have first-hand experience with at least half the negative impacts Brod details.

On the negative side, in this author's experience, there have been early retirements brought on, at least in part, by an inability to adjust to the changing automated environment. Some staff members have used sick leave to rest wrists and arms diagnosed as affected by carpal-tunnel syndrome and to recover from work-related back-strain and fatigue. Cataloging staff have requested that they not be interrupted while at an OCLC terminal because of the increased errors that occur as a result. Office Assistant productivity is regularly assessed according to the number of titles searched or edited in the OCLC system.

As Brod indicates, after automation there is also a greater dependence on specialized, technical skill. Computer operators and systems librarians now regularly appear on the organization charts of automated libraries. However, library automation impacts so many library functions that it is necessary to train virtually every staff member to be technically skilled, at least within a range of activity. This lessens the difficulty of moving staff from job to job. Cross-training and temporary exchanges between staff of different work units can also broaden job knowledge and improve job satisfaction.

Heavy computer use does not inevitably lead to ill-health. Attention to ergonomics and regular breaks from on-terminal work can ease the negative physical impact.

In this author's experience automation has done more to socialize than to isolate library workers. Prior to automation it was possible for each section and branch of the library to operate more or less independently. Training could take place one-on-one between supervisor and supervisee. Unit chiefs could more or less effectively manage in autocratic, unilateral fashion.

Automation necessitates that all policies and procedures be analyzed and recombined in a way that works best for the majority, given the parameters of the automated system. The only effective way to gather the necessary information and to deal with the necessary changes is to involve a broad cross-section of staff in the decision-making process. Once an integrated library system is in place shared files make it impossible for section supervisors to operate autocratically. Procedures and files are in the open in the online system and impact everyone.

The advent of electronic mail revolutionizes the communication process. E-mail makes it more practical to gather advice from a broad range of staff members and to bring staff into the decision-making process even at the clerical level. In order to keep pace with constantly changing procedures and to gather input prior to making decisions impacting circulation of library materials a Circulation Assistant from each Stockton-San Joaquin County Public Library outlet has been made a part of an online circulation liaison network. Each is expected to check for electronic messages from those on the circulation liaison E-mail bulletin board and to respond when ideas are being sought. Each is expected to share information with other staff members in their branches or sections. Electronic mail is an essential key to fast and effective communication in an automated library.

As part of the planning process prior to going online, technical services staff should be asked to assess their job duties and the steps they performed in the total workflow process. They should be involved in the process of restructuring workflow within the new automated environment. Involving staff at all levels helps to take the mystery and the fear out of this massive change process. Regular staff meetings at sectional, divisional, inter-divisional, and library

departmental levels should offer opportunities for staff to participate in planning and implementation of various aspects of the automation process, to provide feedback and recommend changes to
procedure, and to generally remain updated on the changes automation will bring.

Ad hoc task forces of technical and public service staff at various
classification levels should study and make recommendations on
specific projects. In the course of automating, Stockton-San Joaquin
County Public Library has called into action task forces to reorganize circulation policy and procedure, to implement the automated
circulation system, to recommend online catalog implementation
policies and procedures, and to identify manual reference files to be
converted to online databases. Other libraries have experimented
with quality circles to provide the creative input to improve productivity and to implement needed change.[16]

Cribben presents a number of ideas to maximize the effectiveness
of change.[17] All should be kept in mind as an automation project is
implemented. Plan all changes in advance. Build on the strengths of
the department. Determine just how far the project must go to be
effective and do not go beyond that point too quickly. That is, don't
bite off more than can be chewed at one time. Phase implementation. Get solid support for change from all levels. Don't push people into acceptance. Change will only work when people are able to
"buy into" a new plan of action. Remember that there will be both
rational and irrational reactions to change. Prepare for both kinds.
Plan alternatives in case the chosen plan does not work. Get the
critique of others to make sure the plan is not influenced unduly by
the manager's own personal bias.

Cribben's general rules for effective change when applied to a
library automation project will lead to a smoother implementation
process and greater staff acceptance.

AUTOMATION'S ORGANIZATIONAL IMPACT

Myers' informal survey of automated libraries reveals that no
wide-spread reorganization is taking place as a result of library automation.[18] Theoretically, reorganization based on criteria other
than public and technical service divisions should be more possible

in an automated environment, for file maintenance is online and available to anyone with the appropriate authorization.

No definitive study has examined why organizational structures have generally remained along public and technical services lines, despite automation's impact. Speculation leads to several possible explanations.

Libraries are organic structures. They tend to take on the personalities and follow the competencies of their leadership. Middle managers, in particular, are likely to hold long tenure and influence. Depending on the individuals involved, this may result in inertia and resistance to change, or this may result in a creative blend of skills to most effectively manage the organization.

In libraries where integrated library systems have been planned and implemented by strong managers with automation experience there has been some tendency to integrate within technical services those system-wide functions that are encompassed by the automated system. These include, particularly in medium-sized public libraries, the traditional cataloging, processing and acquisitions, and often also centralized circulation control and automated system management. The major integrated functions and databases within the automated system, in particular those that maintain the catalog and patron files, tend to be managed under one "technical" or "support" division.

Where the strong technical services manager with automation experience is not available, then organizational structure will most likely follow a different pattern. Technical Services will most probably be limited to traditional areas and automation will be handled as a staff function reporting directly to the library head or to another appropriate manager.

Size of library also will impact on the organizational structure.[19] Because of span of control issues and the degree of specialization required to run a large library, the Systems Office is often separate from Technical Services. Small libraries will often acquire automated cataloging services from a processing center. Lower price tags for local automated systems, however, are causing more small libraries to purchase computer systems. The need for individuals with automation background and interest is increasing. The individual recruited for this job may not have the background, interest, nor the need to be assigned to traditional technical services functions, especially in a small library setting.

CHANGING JOB DUTIES

One of the most prevalent changes in public library technical services to come about as a result of automation is a crafting of new job descriptions for staff at all levels.

Paraprofessionals

The role of the paraprofessional has changed dramatically. In the past the Library Assistant/Technical Assistant (LA/LTA) in Technical Services supervised physical processing of materials and oversaw catalog card filing and production. They were often assigned simple cataloging routines for added copy material. Procedures were fairly stable and routine. In Acquisitions the LA/LTA assisted with the production of order lists, placed orders, received shipments, corresponded with book jobbers, and prepared pay authorizations for suppliers of received materials. The LA/LTA in charge of Circulation supervised clerical desk staff and oversaw the considerable "behind-the-scenes" work of preparing overdue statements and request filling, as well as, often, deliveries and sometimes maintenance of locator files for collection rotation.

Following automation the Technical Services LA/LTA became the technical expert on OCLC production, a copy cataloger, and supervisor of clerical staff. The Acquisitions Assistant became the resident expert in the online system order and receipt processes and the supervisor of clerical staff in routine order/receipt online processing. In many public libraries the LA/LTA in charge of Circulation has taken on the role of computer system operator and/or system manager. Often this individual has training responsibilities for automated system activity. In other libraries the advent of automation and the consequential increase in responsibility has led to reclassification of the Circulation Supervisor position to the professional level in recognition of the large supervisory and system-wide responsibility.

Taylor and Roney have gathered job descriptions for paraprofessional library staff from a number of public and academic libraries.[20] These listings confirm the highly complex technical and supervisory skills required of paraprofessionals in many automated libraries.

Going hand-in-hand with the increased level of responsibility at the paraprofessional level should be an increased degree of participation in the decision-making process. In Stockton the Library Assistant in charge of AV cataloging also is a member of the Video Committee for selection of videocassette materials. Library Assistants routinely monitor incoming electronic mail messages to Cataloging and Acquisitions Sections and respond as appropriate. They are called upon to share their ideas for improved procedures and to implement those that seem most promising. They are responsible for catalog quality control in large measure, for they do the majority of bibliographic verification and they routinely produce and update most cataloged materials online.

Clerical Staff

On the other hand, automation has tended to narrow clerical duties in many libraries. There are fewer off-terminal tasks to break up the work day. Online procedures follow specific routines dictated by the computer program. These can be very repetitive, particularly in online order, receipt, item inventory, and labelmaking functions.

Here are several ideas to help improve job satisfaction at the clerical level, despite some narrowing of the basic job tasks in an automated environment:

1. Create a Technical Services Clerical Pool as a separate unit, or through coordination by the supervisory staff of their "home" sections within Technical Services, so that a maximum number of jobs can be shared. During hours clericals are not scheduled for duty at a bibliographic utility or local system terminal they may be assigned to assist in receiving materials or typing pay authorizations for Acquisitions, substituting at the Circulation desk, filing or typing for supervisory staff, assisting with the physical processing of materials, tracking down items being called in for recataloging, or working on statistical recordkeeping. This free-floating arrangement allows the workforce to "go with the flow" so that staff are placed

wherever there are gluts in the workflow pipeline or shortages in public desk coverage.

2. Make sure clerical staff are included in staff meetings and are given input into policies and procedures affecting their work.

3. Give staff as much latitude as possible to determine the order in which they will perform their own work routines.

4. Rotate special or off-terminal assignments every six months to one year. However, allow each staff member to become "in-house" expert for at least one routine. Occasional rotation and cross-training will insure that there will be sufficient backup for all functions.

5. Offer staff exchanges to clericals of one to four weeks in duration so that they may get experience working in other sections or branches. This cross-fertilization fosters creativity and fresh insights into old routines.

6. Avoid work monitoring whenever possible. Workload and performance can be sampled periodically. It should not be necessary to constantly monitor quantitatively those who are beyond a trainee level.

Professionals

A check of job ads in *LJ Hotline* over the past several years indicates that, while the beginning Technical Services professional in academic libraries often faces a narrowing of responsibility in the automated environment, in public libraries the job horizons are expanding.

In academic libraries bibliographic utilities have indeed led cataloging librarians to focus on original cataloging, often within narrow subject or material type specialties. Horny notes that automation has led to the demise of many professional positions in Acquisitions.[21] Those who remain may be subject or format specialists, or department heads.

In public libraries, cataloging tends to be tailored more to local need. Professionals continue to work with significant amounts of "copy" cataloging in order to add Dewey Decimal Classification numbers to bibliographic utility contributed copy, or to change numbers that do not conform to the shelf locations desired by that particular library.[22] In some cases, following the lead of Hennepin County Library, catch titles, local subject headings, and cross-references are added to improve bibliographic access to the collection.

The advent of an online catalog and authority control system makes this tailoring of the catalog record all the more possible and useful. The Cataloger/Database Manager in an automated environment, and particularly in a public library setting, may have the opportunity to become the new "renaissance" librarian, quite contrary to Brod's view of the technocrat. It is insufficient to simply have a thorough grasp of cataloging rules and input standards to be a good cataloger in an automated environment. To mold the online public access catalog into a responsive tool the cataloger must also be a good student of high interest topics and a good communicator.

The new Technical Services Librarian within the automated environment must be in full partnership with public services staff in order to do the job effectively. As Database Manager and trainer for use of the online public access catalog, the Technical Services Librarian must become a student of the way the public uses the catalog and the kinds of access points needed.

Cataloging background and a knowledge of database management also makes the Technical Services Librarian a logical choice for leadership in the conversion of various reference files to machine-readable format.[23] These may include community information and referral records, consumer information, local history files, government depository collection records, telephone directory, newspaper, or song title indexes, and a variety of other files.

The Catalog Librarian will be involved in a variety of system-wide activities as technical services liaison to various public service groups and as a member of task forces that are preparing the way for a public access catalog, reference database input, or other projects. The librarian primarily responsible for cataloging children's materials should be a regular attendee at Children's Services meetings and should have the opportunity to work occasionally on the desk in the Children's Section. The librarian primarily responsible for cataloging adult materials should have a liaison role with Adult Services librarians and should have the opportunity to work the Reference Desk. The individual(s) responsible for foreign language cataloging should have input to the development of this collection and materials selection.

The Acquisitions Librarian's professional role is enhanced with automation. Automated fund accounting yields statistics on vendor performance which improves the ability to make informed decisions on where materials dollars will be spent. Collection management reports can put the Acquisitions Librarian in the forefront in analyzing the make-up of the collection and recommending replacement material to fill gaps. Automation provides the electronic communication means for the Acquisitions Librarian to coordinate the selection, order, and receipt process.

Automation makes it possible to look at Acquisitions, Cataloging, and Processing as one materials handling workflow. In libraries with staff sizes of approximately 12 FTE or less handling these functions it makes sense to place one Supervising Librarian in charge of all these functions. Such a position was recently created at Solano County Library in California. While most of Solano County Library's cataloging is produced at a regional processing center, the Supervising Librarian is expected to catalog and classify material as necessary, act as liaison with the processing center, and supervise staff in collection development, order, receipt, and materials processing activities. This individual acts as the assistant to the Technical Services Division head. This frees the Coordinator from day to day supervisory functions in order to focus on automation and other major project planning and implementation responsibilities.

Where staff size or the nature of the responsibilities dictate separate Acquisitions and Cataloging units, there must be a redoubled effort to operate the two units as one team. Unit managers must regularly attend the staff meetings of the other section and there must be daily interaction to make sure that the materials handling pipeline remains free from clogs and dry periods. Many workflow decisions must be coordinated. Here is a small sample:

— whether pre-order searching will be performed in Cataloging or Acquisitions;
— whether Order Records will be entered in full-MARC format, downloaded from a bibliographic utility or entered in brief for-

mat from reviews and publisher's blurbs; who will maintain quality control for records entered online?
— whether partial shipments shall be sent to Cataloging or held for the completion of the order;
— how materials entered online "on-the-fly" will be assessed for discard or inclusion in fully cataloged format;
— whether approval plan materials will be cataloged and available for request online prior to an order meeting or order of added copies, or after all copies have been received; and,
— where a specific title with more than one possible call number will best fit collection needs.

While many of these questions were also present prior to automation, the shared database has made the linkage that much more imperative. A team management approach within Technical Services can work effectively to resolve the many inter-sectional questions and concerns that arise with the installation of an integrated library system.

The Systems Manager will be responsible for day to day supervision of the automated system. He/she will supervise computer operators, prepare functional documentation, and train staff for automated system functions. The Systems Librarian will participate in automated system user group meetings, trouble-shoot software problems, and communicate with both vendor and staff on these concerns. If this individual is also responsible for on- and/or off-desk circulation functions there will be an added supervisory and training load, as well as direct public contact. Again, as a result of automation, here is a technical position which requires the "renaissance" person, someone who is at the same time analytically and technically oriented, and good with people.

SUMMARY

Automation in Technical Services does take its toll in human terms. Some individuals will be unable to take the stress of constant change and of increased need for excellent interpersonal skills. Poor environmental conditions can lead to higher absenteeism and turnover. Narrowed roles at the lower levels may also lead to lowered job satisfaction.

While automation presents problems, it also brings opportunities. Contrary to the picture of the isolated computer technocrat, the Technical Services paraprofessional and professional can look forward to broadened horizons, increased responsibility, and a more central, visible role within the library organization.

If Technical Services staff are to be effective in the automated environment it is required that truly "renaissance" individuals be attracted to the field. The ideal job ad for the Technical Services professional in the typical automated public library might read:

> TECHNICAL SERVICES LIBRARIAN: Wanted—a "renaissance" individual with experience in planning and implementing integrated library systems and with excellent analytical/planning skills to manage computer system operations and those library system-wide materials handling functions of acquisitions, cataloging, processing, and circulation. Acts as database manager for online catalog, I & R and reference index files in computer system. Must be familiar with AACR2, MARC format, bibliographic utility input standards, Open Systems Interconnect networking standards, and other related ANSI standards. Supervises Technical Services units, recommends policy and procedure, and drafts appropriate documentation. Trains library staff in automated functions and communicates concerning system needs with staff and to vendors. Member of Library Management Team. Requires outstanding technical *and* people skills. Must write and speak effectively. Must have training and supervisory experience. Financial management skills, political savvy, and contract negotiation experience are plusses.

NOTES

1. Janet Swan Hill, "Staffing Technical Services in 1995," in *Library Management and Technical Services: The Changing Role of Technical Services in Library Organizations*, Jennifer Cargill, ed. (New York: The Haworth Press, 1988), p. 87-103.

2. Dana C. Rooks and Linda L. Thompson, "Impact of Automation on

Technical Services," in *Library Management and Technical Services: The Changing Role of Technical Services in Library Organizations*, Jennifer Cargill, ed. (New York: The Haworth Press, 1988), p. 121-136.

3. Clinic on Library Applications of Data Processing, (Papers presented at the 22nd Annual Clinic on Library Applications of Data Processing, April 14-16, 1985), *Human Aspects of Library Automation: Helping Staff and Patrons Cope*, Debora Shaw, ed. (Urbana-Champaign: University of Illinois Graduate School of Library and Information Science, 1986).

4. Association of Research Libraries, Office of Management Studies, *Automation and Reorganization of Technical and Public Services*. Spec Kit 112 (Washington, D.C.: ARL, 1985).

5. Maurice J. Freedman, "Automation and the Future of Technical Services," *Library Journal* 109 (June 15, 1984): 1197-1203.

6. Kenneth E. Dowlin, *The Electronic Library* (New York: Neal-Schuman Publishers, 1984).

7. Elizabeth Dickinson Nichols, "The Impact of Library Automation: A Public Librarian's Perspective," *North Carolina Libraries* 45 (Winter 1987): 194-201. See also Elizabeth Dickinson Nichols, "Changing Roles, Changing Job Descriptions in Technical Services," *Library Personnel News* 2 (Winter 1988): 5-6.

8. Lizbeth J. Bishoff, "Who Says We Don't Need Catalogers?" *American Libraries* 18 (September 1987): 694-6.

9. Sheryl Nichin, "Automation's Impact on Technical Services: Increased Professionalism and More Pay," *Illinois Libraries* 65 (May 1983): 299-301.

10. Margaret Myers, "Personnel Considerations in Library Automation," in *The Human Aspects of Library Automation: Helping Staff and Patrons Cope*, Debora Shaw, ed. (Urbana-Champaign: Graduate School of Library and Information Science, 1986), p. 37.

11. Lester Cock and John R. P. French, Jr., "Overcoming Resistance to Change," in *Group Dynamics: Research and Theory*, 3rd ed., Dorwin Cartwright and Alvin Zander, eds. (New York: Harper & Row, 1968), p. 336-50.

12. Ellen Bernstein and John Leach, "Plateau," *American Libraries* 16 (March 1985): 178-80.

13. Renee Feinberg, "Job Satisfaction," *Library Personnel News* 1 (Summer 1987): 21.

14. Craig Brod, *Technostress: The Human Cost of the Computer Generation* (Reading, Massachusetts: Addison-Wesley, 1984).

15. *Ibid*, p. 40-51.

16. Janice DeSirey et al., "The Quality Circle: Catalyst for Library Change," *Library Journal* 113 (April 15, 1988): 52-3.

17. James J. Cribben, *Effective Managerial Leadership* (New York: American Management Association, 1972), p. 253-8.

18. Myers, *op. cit.*, p. 31-2.

19. Hill, *op. cit.*, p. 89-90.

20. Richard L. Taylor and Raymond G. Roney, eds., *Job Descriptions for*

Library Support Personnel (Cleveland, Ohio: Council on Library/Media Technicians, 1985).

21. Karen L. Horny, "Fifteen Years of Automation: Evolution of Technical Services Staffing," *Library Resources and Technical Services* 31 (January/March 1987): 72.

22. Elizabeth D. Nichols and Jennifer Younger, "Library Materials Classification Decision Making Survey: A Study for the ALA/RTSD Classification Institutes" (September 6, 1986).

23. Bishoff, *op. cit.* p. 694-6.

Caught in the Middle:
Systems, Staff and Maintenance in the Medium-Sized Academic Library

Darla H. Rushing

The history of automation in libraries is beginning to be written. Libraries now have ten, fifteen and, in some cases, twenty or more years of experience with computers. Since the beginning of the relationship between libraries and their machines, the effects on staffing patterns caused by those machines has been a favorite topic for speculation and scrutiny.

Because technical services applications were the first to be automated, that is where most scrutiny has occurred. There is no doubt that technical services operations have been transformed by automation. Most histories of the transformation, however, are being written out of the experiences of large academic libraries. Two recent articles of note are Horny's very thorough description of the experiences at Northwestern University,[1] and Andrews' and Kelley's equally interesting report of the Texas Tech experience.[2] Although the emphases are different, i.e., Horney's on actual monetary savings in salaries of both professional and support staff positions, and Andrews' and Kelley's on the upward movement in both responsibility and classification of library assistants, both report substantial reductions in the numbers of technical services staff in the past fifteen years. These histories and others not only document that more is being done with less, but that more-and-better is being done with less.

Do these patterns necessarily follow in other types of libraries?

Darla H. Rushing is Head of Cataloging, Loyola University, New Orleans, LA.

One category of libraries that has received relatively little attention is the medium-sized academic library. A study was made of seven libraries having book holdings in the 250,000- to 600,000-volume range to determine to what degree automation of technical services has affected staffing patterns in the medium-sized academic library. The libraries that participated in the study are: Reinert-Alumni Memorial Library, Creighton University, Omaha, Nebraska; DePaul University Library, Chicago, Illinois; Loyola University Library, New Orleans, Louisiana; Pepperdine University Library, Malibu, California; DuPont-Ball Library, Stetson University, DeLand, Florida; Trinity University Library, San Antonio, Texas; and, Boatwright Memorial Library, the University of Richmond, Richmond, Virginia.

The parent institutions of these libraries are "comprehensive" universities, AAUP category IIA.³ The institutions share these features: they are private, and they have at least one professional school and/or graduate division. Although neither of these characteristics in and of itself might necessarily distinguish these libraries from other libraries in the medium-sized range, taken together they imply certain traits about the institutions and about the constituencies that make up the library user populations. Typically, the faculty and students of such institutions expect from their libraries most of the same qualities found in and services offered by larger academic libraries.

In this atmosphere of high expectation, the comprehensive university library faces the same problems that all libraries face in the last quarter of the 20th century—resources inadequate to, or, if the library is fortunate, stretched by the demands of its users and even by those very machines that have brought about transformations in the delivery of library services. Aside from answering the question about what has happened in technical services staffing during the last decade for this type of library, the study further intended to discover what issues and problems the medium-sized academic library encounters as it installs a local library system, and to what degree the operation and maintenance of that system will require yet another re-evaluation of staffing needs.

A survey format was chosen, and a set of questions was posed to the heads of technical services (or to the individual whose position most closely fits that description) at the seven selected libraries. The respondents were interviewed by telephone in April of 1989. While this method insured a 100% return, it also encouraged a more free response than a written questionnaire might have allowed. A response, "We feel that . . .," did not always result in quantifiable data. Indeed, some of the questions were phrased in terms of, "Do you perceive that . . .?" (See the Appendix for the complete questionnaire.)

The participating libraries were questioned about current staffing patterns and changes over the past ten years, or since the automation of cataloging; current status of automation, including systems employed; attitudes toward and practices regarding catalog maintenance before and after automation; authority control before and after automation; and the problems of territoriality in automated systems when multiple users, both library departments and other libraries, are involved.

AUTOMATION OF TECHNICAL SERVICES: HISTORY AND CHANGE

Of the libraries surveyed, Trinity University Library has had the longest experience with automation. During the late 1960s and early 1970s, in a joint venture with the university's computer center, Trinity designed and developed an automated batch cataloging system that eventually became MARCIVE. The university subsequently joined OCLC. All other libraries are OCLC users with memberships ranging in duration from five to fifteen years. In all cases, cataloging was the first of the technical services functions to be automated.

Respondents were asked to discuss changes in numbers and levels of staff over the last ten years, or since the automation of cataloging. Like their larger counterparts, three libraries reported that the automation of cataloging has resulted in staff reductions. Three other libraries, however, have actually added staff in technical services during the past decade. In one of these latter cases, the growth was in direct response to automation, when the opportunity came about to bring bibliographic control and catalog access to branch libraries and previously uncataloged collections.

Whether a library added or deleted staff, a common experience among these six libraries was the rearrangement of staff among the various technical services units and a realignment of duties. Only one library, Pepperdine, reported no changes either in numbers or arrangement of technical services staff. The fact that four of the seven libraries reported no change or, more surprisingly, growth in technical services implies that the economies of scale of some technical services operations might provide more opportunity for staff reductions in large libraries than those same operations might provide in the medium-sized library. A further implication might be that medium-sized academic libraries, specifically those in comprehensive universities, have taken advantage in significant ways of the computer's ability to perform tasks better, but, in terms of staffing expenditures, not necessarily more inexpensively.

The DePaul University Library most closely follows the large-library patterns reported in the literature. Since 1979 one of six professional positions and two of thirteen clerical positions have been reassigned to public services. DePaul reports that this was as much due to a critical need in public services because of significant growth in student enrollment as to substantially reduced technical services needs. DePaul's remarkable enrollment growth, making it the largest institution of the seven, is now being matched by increases in the library materials budgets, thereby creating renewed staffing pressure in the technical services departments.

At Creighton University one of three paraprofessional positions was eliminated, and at the University of Richmond one of four professional staff positions was eliminated. But Richmond also reported adding the Music Library to its realm of cataloging responsibility, with the Music Librarian assigned to cataloging half time. The net loss then becomes one half-time professional position of four.

Stetson reported that increasing automation responsibilities made it difficult for the head of technical services to continue as senior cataloger, and an additional nine-month cataloging position was added. A separate serials department was consolidated with technical services, the professional serials position moved to reference, and a support staff position substituted in the formerly professional position. Streamlining serials required further automation. In total staff changes technical services gained 1.75 positions. The rearrangement and realignment illustrated a trend at Stetson to increase support staff in technical services as automation permits the move of professional staff to public services positions.

During the pre-automation era at Loyola University, only brief cataloging had been done for music and sound recordings in the music library and for audiovisual materials in the media center. Since full cataloging for both of these collections was viewed as desirable, a professional music/a-v cataloger was added to the one existing professional position in cataloging. The automation of acquisitions and the inclusion of the music library in this operation resulted in one half-time clerical position added to an acquisitions staff of three. In the serials department, changes in the responsibilities of the professional position, the automation of serials, and the inclusion of the music library serials acquisition and processing required the addition of a second full-time clerical position. Student assistants have been added for data entry in cataloging (3FTE), and for binding in acquisitions (1FTE). While some of these additions must be tied to a modest growth in library materials budgets, Loyola provides a good example of the medium-sized academic library that has significantly improved services through the use of modern library technology.

The Trinity University Library is an even more notable exception to the pattern of staff reductions. The library has been a major focus for the university's plan for general institutional improvement, and in the late 1970s and early 1980s there were substantial increases in monies for library collection development. Fortunately, the Trinity administration has been able to support collection development with staffing resources. There have been fluctuations in staffing, as positions have been added to catalog and process the new acquisitions, and then deleted as the materials budgets have stabilized. The additions included seven positions in cataloging and five positions in acquisitions, some of which have been shifted to public services. Even with the remarkable growing spurt having levelled off, the technical services staff at Trinity is approximately a third larger than it was ten years ago. While the technical services staff at Trinity has grown markedly, the acquisition rate has quadrupled, from ten thousand to forty thousand volumes per year. Trinity is an example of a library whose character and mission have been altered by changes in its parent institution. Obviously, these kinds of alterations cannot be credited to automation, but automation has enabled libraries such as Trinity to deal with them efficiently, providing that collection development resources have been matched with an appropriate level of personnel and equipment resources.

RESPONSIBILITY FOR SYSTEMS: STAFFING PATTERNS

In general, automation efforts in medium-sized academic libraries, like those in large research libraries, have originated in technical services departments and in cataloging departments in particular. As these libraries have begun to install local systems, however, a major staffing pattern difference between them and their larger counterparts can be observed. In large libraries there is almost always a systems librarian or manager who is often assisted by a number of staff committed to the support of computer hardware, software and operations. Of the seven medium-sized academic libraries in this study none has a "systems department" *per se*, headed by a systems librarian. Rather, in all but one institution, technical services includes systems operations. In five of those six, the head of technical services serves as systems librarian. At the University of Richmond a cataloger with skills and interest in automation has become systems librarian. It is planned that she will continue her responsibilities for audio visual cataloging. Loyola is exceptional in that its "system coordinator" is the head of circulation.

Karen Horny alludes to the fact that, in large libraries, savings from technical services staff reductions may have been more than consumed by the birth and growth of systems departments, but also argues that, when online public access catalogs and their linked circulation systems are integrated, it is difficult to assess the division of costs.' In medium-sized libraries, at least in this sample, the non-existence of separate systems departments may be the point at which these libraries have realized staff savings. The assumption on the part of libraries and their managers seems to have been that with the availability of so-called turn-key systems, the employment of full-time staff for systems operation is unnecessary. Also, the precedent for multiple-responsibility positions in the medium-sized academic library may have fostered the development of this staffing pattern. In a later section evidence will be presented that this particular staffing pattern may lead to problems of territoriality.

CURRENTLY USED SYSTEMS: THE AUTOMATION MARKETPLACE TAKEN TO ITS ULTIMATE CONCLUSION

In the past there has been some discussion in library automation circles about the problem of standardization, both of hardware and software. This problem might appropriately be raised as a serious concern, as systems in the selected libraries are examined. With vendors emerging and subsequently disappearing from the marketplace, the ease with which a library might move from one vendor to another, taking its expensively created database intact, becomes an issue that is apparent simply by looking at the systems and vendors chosen by the seven libraries. This sample of medium-sized academic libraries reveals great diversity in approaches to the automation of technical services functions.

Pepperdine has had a VTLS system installed on its two campuses since September 1985, using online public access catalog, circulation, and serials control modules, although serials data are not yet complete. Creighton University is a PALS library, with the system shared among health sciences, law and main libraries. DePaul has participated since 1987 in a cooperative system, LCS,[5] shared among thirty-three Illinois libraries, that provides online public access catalog, circulation and interlibrary loan functions. Loyola University began using CLSI for circulation control in 1980 in its main and branch libraries, but not its law library. The installation of an upgrade in 1988 added an online public access catalog module. Trinity has used CLSI for circulation since 1979, while a COM (film and fiche) public catalog is produced bimonthly from tapes of OCLC and Marcive records. Stetson uses a Bibliofile CD-ROM online public access catalog that is updated monthly. The University of Richmond has recently signed a contract with Dynix to provide online public access catalog and circulation/reserve book room modules, with acquisitions, media booking, and serials function to be added at a later time.

A similar variegated pattern exists in the choice of serials control and acquisitions systems as well. Pepperdine, with its VTLS system, is the only library surveyed that presently includes a serials module in its local system. All other libraries have stand-alone serials control systems: OCLC SC350 (Richmond); EBSCO's pc-based system (Creighton); Checkmate, a pc-based system (Loyola); Innovative Interfaces systems for both acquisitions and serials control (DePaul); and a locally developed D-base system for acquisitions, serials holdings and accounting (Stetson). Other systems in use for acquisitions include Ballin's BALLINET and BIP on CD-ROM (Richmond); Baker & Taylor's online system (Creighton); and OCLC ACQ350 (Loyola). Some libraries reported continued use of manual systems for various processes. In one case, Trinity University, an automated acquisitions system was eliminated and the library returned to a manual system for monograph acquisitions, since the automated system was not particularly useful in the context of Trinity's accelerated acquisitions program.

Of all the possible combinations only Loyola and Trinity use a common vendor for one function — circulation — and in that instance the systems are functionally dissimilar since Loyola's upgrade. This amazing variety illustrates the ongoing fluidity in the library systems marketplace. It also illustrates that, for medium-sized academic libraries, most of whom buy off-the-shelf-products, the truly integrated system is not yet a reality.

CATALOG MAINTENANCE: ATTITUDES BEFORE AND AFTER AUTOMATION

Before automation the medium-sized academic library's attitudes toward catalog maintenance and authority control might best be described as uneven. Some libraries reported that in the pre-automation past there was not enough staff or time to perform in-depth catalog maintenance. Actions taken on changes reported from the Library of Congress were described by one library as "hit or miss," and this was a fairly typical answer to the pre-automation maintenance questions.

Authority files, if they existed, were generally not as sophisticated as those found in large academic libraries. Usually the card
catalog itself served as the library's authority file for name headings, while the catalog or the Library of Congress Subject Headings, "the red book," served as the library's subject authority file.
Local headings for both names and subjects were maintained in the
card catalog or as notes in "the red book." Series authority files
were maintained by four of the libraries surveyed.

The advent of network cataloging presented for the medium-
sized academic library yet another maintenance problem in yet another "catalog" where maintenance needed to be done. Several
libraries reported that there was some inconsistency with regard to
their maintenance of these "unseen, unknown" databases. DePaul,
Pepperdine and Richmond, however, reported that catalog maintenance had been a very high priority before automation and throughout the period of online cataloging prior to the installation of local
systems. Similarly, Stetson reported that a reclassification/retro-
spective conversion project had enabled them to come to a high
level of database accuracy.

Those libraries where integrated library systems are in place with
online public access catalogs operational all reported increased
staffing needs specifically caused by catalog maintenance requirements. Creighton will add back one paraprofessional position for
full-time catalog maintenance. Pepperdine reports a need for more
staff for this purpose, but no immediate prospects for additions.
Loyola hopes to add a half-time clerical position. With a combina-
tion of Trinity's increases in staff and reassignments of responsibilities, two staff positions plus one professional librarian are now ded-
icated to full-time catalog maintenance and authority work.

At DePaul the LCS membership results in a different kind of
complexity in catalog maintenance.[6] The first entry of a record into
the LCS union catalog becomes the master record, and there is no
locally-edited cataloging record available online to individual members, much the same as the situation with an OCLC master record.
Since a number of participants in LCS are public libraries that do
brief or even incomplete cataloging, upgrading records for the academic library participants in LCS is considered a very high priority.
There is a seven-member users' group that is authorized to make

changes to bibliographic records and to create authority records. Each member of the group is required to have two staff persons trained for maintenance activities and is asked to contribute between ten and twenty hours per week toward record upgrade. The changes can be made only via batch process, not online.

All libraries agreed that catalog maintenance in automated systems, especially those featuring online public access catalogs, must be addressed on a continuous and consistent basis. The evidence shows that libraries are willing to dedicate substantial portions of their technical services resources to this activity. And, consistent with Janet Swan Hill's prediction that the level of staff required for database maintenance and authority work will rise,[7] the seven libraries reported this as a pattern already in place.

CATALOG MAINTENANCE:
METHOD BROUGHT TO MADNESS

In manual catalogs the revision of card filing was a principal means of detecting errors. In automated systems errors can easily enter the files undetected. Even when authority control is in place, there is the possibility of errors in those indexed fields not affected by its imposition. As yet, no system provides a spelling check type of feature. The way that errors are identified for corrections must necessarily combine human and machine intervention.

Most libraries rely heavily on reference departments as a source of information about potential problems and for recommendations for changes. But no library surveyed has reference librarians actually making changes on line. Catalog maintenance is still viewed as a cataloging department function, and most maintenance activities are carried out by professional catalogers or experienced paraprofessional staff with clerical assistance. Policymaking is generally a cataloging department group effort with final authority for decision-making resting with the head of technical services.

Authority files are seen as essential in the online environment by all libraries surveyed. This finding is consistent with that of Baer and Johnson in their recent work.[8] Authority files are one area where standardization from catalog to catalog is occurring, as most libraries accept authority records from the Library of Congress or from the vendors that supply LC authority records. Medium-sized libraries have abandoned most attempts at transferring local manual authority files, no matter how relevant to local practice, into their online systems. Loyola does report some efforts in the area of local subject authority work for its special collection of Louisiana music and sound recordings, but also reports that the CLSI manual authority record creation is quite cumbersome. At this point it is worth noting that no library surveyed reported having interface capability for downloading authority records from OCLC into its local system, although this will be a feature of Richmond's Dynix system. With authority control modules still in relatively primitive states, it might be wise to refer to Taylor, Maxwell, and Frost's "questions . . . in considering vendor systems,"[9] and ask a few more such as, "Does the vendor provide for downloading authority records from a bibliographic utility?"

Pepperdine is the only library surveyed where systematic daily maintenance of authority files and linked bibliographic records is being done. Input of new or changed authority records is a manual process, but this labor-intensive activity is viewed as appropriate since the VTLS system does accommodate global change. In other systems where global change capability is not yet available there is generally no attempt made to systematically review and update authority records. Libraries are relying on tape-loading of records from vendors. Trinity University comments that it has been satisfied with its bimonthly tape processing for many years and points to this method's significant labor-saving advantages, also to better control of the data since working with files rather than record-by-record can produce a higher level of accuracy.

An obvious disadvantage to the batch processing of records is timeliness in the authorization of headings and in the creation of references. Also, while the labor-saving advantages are significant the costs of ongoing tape subscriptions and processing are also and must be considered when planning for the overall cost of system maintenance.

In considering the allocation of personnel and operational resources a library must determine to what extent the library's constituents require accuracy in the catalog. Even in the atmosphere of high expectation some kinds of catalog maintenance or lack of same are not apparent to users. Of course, non-retrieval is not necessarily apparent to users either, but that would negate the very purpose of the catalog. In any event, it is interesting to note that, in answer to a survey question regarding changes in their attitudes toward maintenance of automated systems, libraries perceived the increased need for catalog maintenance to be more often system-driven than user-driven.

WHOSE BABY IS IT ANYWAY?
THE ISSUE OF TERRITORIALITY

Few medium-sized academic libraries are well along the road toward the totally integrated library. As we have already seen, just the opposite is true: libraries are struggling along with a variety of systems and are doing their best with limited resources to figure out how to make them work efficiently. However, in those situations where more than one function is served by a local system, problems of territoriality can and do occur, and this may become more evident as more functions are added. Some problems seem likely to happen if the equipment itself resides in the computer center or at some other off-site location.

Perhaps "coordination problems" would be a more appropriate phrase than "problems of territoriality," as described by DePaul and Creighton. DePaul reports that the complexity of LCS and the uneven quality of bibliographic records has made for system-wide difficulties. At Creighton the needs of the main library have perhaps been subordinated to the needs of the medical library, where PALS was first installed, even though the main library's collection is larger. Furthermore, the equipment itself is housed in the university's computer center. Creighton describes itself as still in the initial implementation stages, and assumes that further developments will alleviate coordination difficulties.

Responsibility for data entry is a second point at which difficulties can arise. In comparing the only commonly used system, data entry has been handled differently. Trinity and Loyola have each had CLSI circulation systems for many years. At Trinity all data entry and database maintenance is and has been performed by technical services staff. In Loyola's case the greatest responsibility for data entry was formerly assigned to the circulation department. With an upgrade to a full MARC record capability and the addition of an online public access catalog module, the cataloging department has become primarily responsible for the creation and maintenance of the database. Since copy specific information and also retrospective conversion are incomplete, some coordination problems occur. The circulation department continues to add retrospective copy specific data and the cataloging department adds new bibliographic records and holdings. In all other libraries the technical services staff does all data entry.

Technical services staff continue to have a highly refined proprietary interest in the contents of the system's bibliographic and holdings data. But the catalog, once considered the domain of technical services staff, is coming to be viewed even more than ever as a public services tool. This phenomenon is probably due to two factors: the necessity for more in-depth instruction in the use of the automated catalog, and the similarity in the techniques for effective searching of an online public access catalog and those used by reference librarians in database searching. Conversely, catalog use studies, once conducted by the reference staff are now often generated as system reports, making this particular arena of library activity appear to switch from public to technical services.

The recently formed symbiotic relationship between public and technical services, or perhaps more properly, between each of these and its host, the system, causes a certain amount of unhealthy competition. In the medium-sized academic library, the perception of inequality among library departments exists, whether or not the reality does.

In the first situation, where a system is shared among users, coordination and diplomacy are the keys to success. In the second situation, where the problems are intra-library, the most obvious solution is to have a full-time systems librarian who is not attached to any one department and whose office is located in a neutral zone. If systems operation does not require 100% of the work day for this individual, other duties might include responsibility for other kinds of library technologies. Ideally, such a person would take initiatives for implementing new technologies and could serve as an in-house reference source for the entire library. From a management perspective, great care should be exercised to avoid perceptions of inequality among both groups of libraries and library departments.

CONCLUSIONS

Staffing patterns in medium-sized academic libraries do not exhibit universal or significant downward trends as a result of automation. Integrated systems are virtually non-existent in this type and size of library. In fact, "fragmentation" rather than "integration" would be a more accurate descriptor. Although systems are evolving quickly, there is not yet a move toward standardization, nor toward a set of workable interfaces between or among systems. Library automation is still a very unsettled business, and as a consequence, complex management issues remain.

As the libraries begin to install systems with a certain degree of integration, two problems become evident: libraries see their staffing needs increasing with the requirements for database maintenance; and libraries are experiencing difficulties with coordination and sometimes, more seriously, territoriality, when more than one library or group requires use of a system. The problems reported from medium-sized academic libraries may be handled more easily at larger, or possibly even smaller, libraries. As the examples given suggest, diplomatic and creative management can resolve these problems.

While libraries are appropriately proud of their increased productivity and their efforts at providing excellent access to their collections, they perceive that user expectations may be outpacing their ability to respond. For the medium-sized academic library there is a good deal of uncertainty and anxiety about how to deliver the best access to information that money can buy within the limitations of its staff and equipment budgets. In answer to the question, "Is your library past the crisis point in its automation efforts, or do you feel that you are still on the critical list?" only two of the seven libraries surveyed replied positively to the former. However, this does hold out hope for the others and for all libraries, where bigger is not necessarily better.

NOTES

1. Karen L. Horny, "Fifteen Years of Automation: Evolution of Technical Services Staffing," *Library Resources & Technical Services* 31 (Jan-Mar 1987):69-76.

2. Virginia Lee Andrews and Carol Marie Kelley, "Changing Staffing Patterns in Technical Services Since the 1970s: A Study in Change," *Journal of Library Administration* 9 (no. 1, 1988):55-70.

3. For a definition of Category IIA, "comprehensive institutions," see *Academe* 75 (Mar-Apr 1989), p. 20.

4. Horny, "Fifteen Years of Automation," p. 76.

5. A detailed description of LCS as implemented at the University of Illinois at Urbana-Champaign is found in "Special Section: In Depth—The Online Catalogue of the University of Illinois at Urbana-Champaign," *Information and Technology and Libraries* 4 (Dec 1985): 306-351.

6. Ibid., pp. 324-338, for details of catalog maintenance procedures of LCS in the sub-section "Maintenance of an Online Catalog," by Sharon E. Clark and Winnie Chan.

7. Janet Swan Hill, "Staffing Technical Services in 1995," *Journal of Library Administration* 9 (no.1, 1988): 97.

8. Nadine L. Baer and Karl E. Johnson, "The State of Authority," *Information Technology and Libraries* 7 (June 1988): 150-151.

9. Arlene G. Taylor, Margaret F. Maxwell, and Carolyn O. Frost, "Network and Vendor Authority Systems," *Library Resources & Technical Services* 29 (Apr-June 1985): 203.

APPENDIX:
Questionnaire

1. Does "technical services" in your library include systems operation?

2. Into what (other) units is technical services divided?

3. What is the current size of your technical services staff? ____ Professionals, ____ Paraprofessionals, ____ Clericals, ____ Students

4. Does this represent any significant change over the past 10 years? ± ____ Professionals, ± ____ Paraprofessionals, ± ____ Clericals, ± ____ Students

5. If there have been changes, are they attributable directly to automation or to some other factor, such as increased or decreased acquisitions?

6. In what areas is your library automated? (Please include "public services" functions.)

7. What are the approximate dates of automation of each of the above?

8. What local systems (if any) do you employ?

9. Has your library engaged in a retrospective conversion project? If yes, how was this carried out?

10. If you used a vendor, what were your requirements for editing? What was the quality of the work? What means have you used for checking quality?

11. Have you employed a vendor for authority control? How successful was the project? What means have you used for checking this?

12. To what degree was catalog maintenance considered important before automation, as opposed to, say, keeping cataloging backlogs under control?

13. To what degree is catalog maintenance considered important post-automation?

14. If there is a change in attitude toward catalog maintenance, do you perceive this to be system-driven or user-driven or both?

15. What kinds of authority systems did you have in place before automation?

16. Does your current automated system employ authority control?

17. If yes, did you transfer local manual authority files to the automated system? By what means?

18. If your system offers authority control, are headings linked to bibliographic records? If yes, do changed authority records result in changed bibliographic headings?

19. How are new authority records created in your system?

20. Who is responsible for the verification of new authority records? for making changes to automated bibliographic and authority records? for the creation of policy regarding authority control and database maintenance?

21. If your system includes serials records, who is responsible for recording serial holdings?

22. If your system includes circulation information, who is responsible for the maintenance of copy specific information?

23. If your system includes "on-order" information, who is responsible for its input?

24. If "on-order" or "in-process" information is displayed in an on-line public access catalog, has this resulted in increased demand for "rush" cataloging?

25. Do you perceive any problems of territoriality or issues of control in any of the above?

26. Is your library past the crisis point in its automation efforts, or do you feel that you are still on the critical list?

Job Satisfaction:
Does Automation Make a Difference?

Leigh Estabrook
Chloe Bird
Frederick L. Gilmore

The infusion of technology into all types of library activity changes the way in which professionals, support staff and library users work. These changes may affect the way staff view their work. Attitudes about work are not stable over time nor do they simply reflect whether a particular employee is a "happy" person. The work environment and the type of job done affect individual attitudes. At a time of rapid change in the use of technology in libraries, one is led to question whether such change affects worker satisfaction. Does technology make a difference on how people feel about their work?

This article examines job satisfaction among professional and support staff members in one private and three public university libraries. In particular, it looks at (1) the factors that contribute significantly to job satisfaction, (2) whether use of technology related significantly to job satisfaction and (3) staff likes and dislikes. Finally, the authors discuss ways in which job satisfaction may change in the future as libraries more fully exploit computer and communications technologies.

Leigh Estabrook is Dean and Professor, Graduate School of Library and Information Science, Chloe Bird is Research Assistant, Department of Sociology, and Frederick L. Gilmore is Research Assistant, Graduate School of Library and Information Science at the University of Illinois at Urbana-Champaign.

The authors are indebted to grants from the Research Board of the University of Illinois and the Association for Library and Information Science that provided support for travel and research assistance.

RESEARCH ON JOB SATISFACTION IN LIBRARIES

Research on job satisfaction in the library labor force dates back to the 1970s, although discussions of employee productivity in the library first appeared in the 1950s.[1] The number of articles on job satisfaction in libraries between 1973 and 1983 indicates the strong interest in the subject in that decade; but since the mid-1980s job satisfaction has received only limited attention and research on the subject has narrowed.[2]

Marchant's initial study of satisfaction among librarians (1970) forms the base for his work on participative management theory in libraries (1976). He found that relations with supervisors, salary increases, client relations and work duties are the best predictors of overall job satisfaction. Bengston and Shields (1985) repeated Marchant's study in a single academic library and found similar relationships between satisfaction and aspects of workers' jobs. Pybril's 1973 study of librarians, clerical workers and service personnel in a large Midwest university does not support these findings. In Pybril's sample of 69 librarians, clerical and service workers, job satisfaction does not vary with job responsibilities or occupational level.

Plate and Stone's (1973) study of 237 self-selected workshop attendees from various types of libraries in the United States and Canada supports the findings of earlier work by Herzberg (1959).[3] Satisfaction and dissatisfaction result from distinct but interrelated agents. Job satisfaction can be explained by the job itself; job dissatisfaction, by the job environment.

Subsequent studies focus on the relationship between personal and organizational characteristics and job satisfaction with contradictory results. D'Elia's 1979 study of 228 recent library school graduates employed in a variety of libraries found no connection between a librarian's gender, the type of library in which he or she works, vocational needs and job satisfaction. In D'Elia's study, supervisory climate and intrinsic job characteristics were the strongest determinants of job satisfaction.

In a comparative analysis of 265 employees in six university libraries, Vaughn and Dunn (1974) found no significant differences in job satisfaction among the libraries studied or among departments within these libraries. Scammel and Stead's (1980) study of job satisfaction among 68 librarians found no differences attributable to age or library experience.[4]

Lynch and Verdin (1983) report results from a 1972 study suggesting that job satisfaction for librarians must be placed within the context of the profession and its own special needs and agenda. They found (1) gender is not related to differences in job satisfaction; (2) younger professionals are less satisfied than their older counterparts; (3) those planning to remain in the same job for the next five years are more satisfied than those who seek upward mobility; (4) department heads are more satisfied than subordinates; (5) librarians in reference are the most satisfied of library workers; and (6) professionals are more satisfied than support staff. In a replication of this study in two of the three libraries, Lynch and Verdin (1987) confirm their original conclusions.

Each of these studies has some limitations (e.g., sample size, source of data, method of analysis, or questions asked). Together they suggest that the work environment and characteristics of the work itself are important determinants of job satisfaction.

RESEARCH ON THE EFFECTS
OF TECHNOLOGY ON JOBS

The importance of work environment and characteristics of work to job satisfaction strongly suggests that technological change may have an effect on job satisfaction in libraries. Although few researchers have examined this relationship, studies suggest that technology affects library staffs' attitudes toward work. For example, a recent study of support staff in three libraries by Jones (1989), reports that a majority of respondents feel working with computers makes their job easier and cite more positive than negative reactions to automation.

An important body of research within other types of organizations examines the impact of technology on the nature of work and on job satisfaction of employees. Their findings are suggestive to researchers in library and information science, but inconclusive. Braverman (1974) first argued that technology affords management increased control over workers and allows, as a consequence, progressive deskilling of work. Noble (1984) expands on this notion in his study of machine-paced work during the 1940s and 50s and Shaiken (1984) argues that the design of new automated systems reflects conscious decisions by management. In an automated workplace, services are integrated, information transfer occurs more quickly, and limitations of time and space decrease. "Departments" lose their identity as the respective activities of the workers move closer together. Shaiken argues that these changes present obstacles to job satisfaction for workers. In his examination of the shift from typing to word processing, Shaiken found that variety, meaning of work, worker contributions, feedback and communication are all reduced for typists who shifted to working on computers.

Form's (1987) review of recent research concludes it is difficult to make meaningful generalizations about the overall effects of automation on work: in some fields automation leads to increased demand for skills; in others, less. Form cautions against predicting the future from past studies.

Similar problems exist in studies of the effect of technology on job satisfaction. Blumberg and Gerwin (1980) studied job satisfaction of workers in a manufacturing system and found them to be more dissatisfied than workers in the general population. They conclude that the manufacturing workers had decreased opportunity to use skills that had been valued prior to automation.

More recently, the National Research Council reviewed research on the effects of technology on the quality of work and concluded:

> These surveys suggest that workers who use information technology are generally satisfied with it, because it allows them to do their work better and because it improves the jobs themselves or, at a minimum, does not degrade them significantly. (Hartmann 1986, p. 134)

It is difficult to hypothesize from existing research how technology may be affecting either the work environment or job satisfaction within libraries because much of it is based on case studies of specific industries or a sample of organizations within a particular type of work. These studies suggest the types of issues that researchers in library and information science should examine (for example, changes in skilling level, in autonomy and social interaction). They do not identify clear trends across work sectors, nor suggest how library staff may be affected.

A STUDY OF LIBRARIANS

This article reports the findings from a study conducted at four academic libraries between June and October, 1988.[5] Librarians and support staff at each library completed a self-administered questionnaire on the staff members work and use of technology.[6,7] After completing the questionnaire, some members of the staff met with Estabrook in small homogeneous groups divided by technical/public services and professional/support staff to consider questions of how technology is changing their work.

Level of job satisfaction is measured by a single question "All things considered, how satisfied are you with your present job?" Responses range from 1 (not very satisfied) to 4 (very satisfied). Demographic variables used as controls include: gender (males are coded 1), race (white is coded 1), and marital status (married is coded 1). Age and education are measured in years. To control for possible differences between libraries, "dummy variables" are included to identify the employing library (coded 1 for the employing library and 0 for all others) of each respondent.

The study also measured "extrinsic" and "intrinsic" rewards of jobs. The extrinsic rewards include income (thousands of dollars per year) and opportunity for advancement (an index based on five questions ranging from 1 (very unlikely) to 4 (very likely).[8] The intrinsic rewards included are: (1) amount of discretion over work (1 = not at all; 4 = a lot); and (2) social integration — an index based on four questions which measure frequency of social interaction with coworkers on breaks and away from the job (5 = almost every day; 1 = seldom or never).

The two independent variables in the study are use of technology measured in hours per day using the computer; and level of job stress (computed from a ten point scale of stress "in your life" multiplied by the percentage of stress reported as job-related). Values range from 0 (no stress) to 10 (a great deal of stress, 100 percent job related). The analysis of job likes and dislikes is based on re-sponses to two questions: (1) Please describe the three things about your job that you like the most; and (2) Please describe the three things about your job that you dislike the most. The sample includes 491 respondents in four libraries. Missing data on some of the variables restricted this analysis to 402 respondents: 153 professionals and 249 support staff. The overall response rate is 63 percent.

FINDINGS

Job Satisfaction

Due to the differences in work conditions for each group, sepa-rate analyses are employed for professionals and support staff. Pro-fessionals and support staff report different levels of overall satis-faction with their present job (see Table 1). In t-tests of group means by professional status, professionals have a significantly higher mean satisfaction level than support staff ($p < .05$) (see Ta-ble 2). Professionals are older, have higher incomes, more educa-tion and are more likely to be male than their support staff counter-parts. There are no significant differences between professionals

TABLE 1. Job Satisfaction for Professional and Support Staff

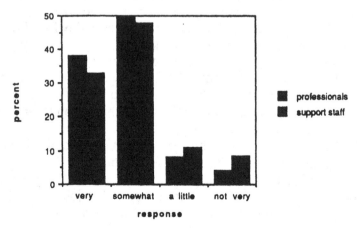

TABLE 2. Means and Standard Deviations of Demographic Characteristics and Job Attributes for Professional and Support Staff

	Professionals	Support Staff
Job Satisfaction	3.209* (.775)	3.072 (.844)
Education	17.908*** (1.574)	15.470 (2.030)
Male	.359*** (.481)	.177 (.382)
Age	45.438*** (9.669)	38.173 (10.459)
Married	.569 (.497)	.542 (.499)
White	.961 (.195)	.960 (.197)
Computer time	1.900*** (1.720)	2.750 (2.434)
Income	32.846*** (10.882)	17.692 (6.216)
Opportunity	2.056** (.709)	2.259 (.768)
Social	2.361 (.758)	2.400 (.785)
Discretion	2.976*** (.533)	2.552 (.588)
Job Stress	4.104*** (2.211)	3.010 (2.179)
Library A	.209* (.408)	.137 (.344)
Library B	.137 (.345)	.205 (.404)
Library C	.392 (.490)	.402 (.491)
Library D	.261 (.441)	.257 (.483)
N	153	249

and support staff in proportion of minorities or married persons across these four libraries. Nor do the two groups differ significantly in amount of social interaction with co-workers. Professionals do report significantly greater job stress and greater discretion over their work. The latter two findings seem consistent with the greater responsibilities placed on professional staff.

Librarians report spending significantly less time using the computer. This is a reflection of the way in which libraries implement new technologies: support operations such as copy cataloging and circulation are the two computerized processes in almost all these libraries, but few librarians have access to a computer terminal at their desk. Support staff indicate somewhat greater opportunity for advancement. This may reflect the specific conditions of the libraries in this study. In three of the four communities in which these libraries are located, there are no other academic libraries. In those situations, support staff may perceive opportunities to move into other employment sectors of the community. Geographically immobile librarians who face a pyramidal organizational structure may have few professional options.

Regression analysis tests the extent to which these variables explain job satisfaction (Table 3). Due to the differences in work and in the reward system for professional and support staff, separate models are employed to explain job satisfaction within each group. These two models explain nearly one-third of the variation in job satisfaction across individuals. Perhaps the most significant finding is that, controlling for other job attributes, use of technology alone does not explain any of the variance in job satisfaction. The only two factors significantly related to satisfaction for both groups are social interaction and job stress; neither of these variables correlates significantly with the amount of time a staff member uses technology. Those people who socialize with co-workers during breaks, lunches and away from work report higher levels of satisfaction with their jobs. Those who report low levels of job stress are more satisfied with their work.

Both professional and support staff at one institution express significantly less satisfaction with their work. While the inclusion of the dummy variables for institution increases the explained variance of the model, it does not affect the model since the same variables

TABLE 3. Regressions of Job Satisfaction on Demographic Characteristics and Job Attributes by Professional Status

	Professionals		Support Staff	
	b	beta	b	beta
White	1.053***	.265	-.230	-.054
Age	.006	.072	.007	.089
Male	-.064	-.040	-.119	-.054
Education	.039	.078	-.112***	-.270
Married	.035	.022	.101	.060
Library A	-.017	-.009	-.090	-.037
Library B	.130	.058	-.209	-.100
Library C	-.296	-.187	-.315*	-.184
Computer time	-.005	-.012	.007	.019
Income	.012*	.165	.010	.073
Opportunity	.129	.118	-.039	-.036
Social	.189**	.185	.113*	.105
Discretion	.071	.049	.409***	.285
Job Stress	-.139***	-.396	-.092***	-.238
Intercept	.624		3.76	
R^2	.326		.298	

* p .05   One-tailed test is used except for library dummy variables, since
** p .01   we made no hypothesis of direction.
*** p .001

remain significant with or without consideration of where an individual works. Although institutions differ in overall level of job satisfaction, the same factors affect satisfaction for personnel in each of the libraries.

Among professional librarians, race is the second largest factor in explaining job satisfaction. Whites are significantly more satisfied with their jobs. This finding is disturbing, for it suggests that libraries do not treat minority workers equally. Other significant factors are income and amount of social interaction with colleagues, both of which are positively associated with higher satisfaction for professionals.

For support staff, the single largest factor affecting job satisfaction is job discretion. The opportunity to determine what work is done and how it is performed contributes positively to individual satisfaction. It seems worth noting that the amount of discretion over work is not similarly related to the job satisfaction of professionals.

Satisfaction of support staff is also negatively related to level of education. This finding is typical for workers who are overeducated for their jobs, but holds particular significance for libraries that often have talented and highly educated personnel in support roles. As Table 2 indicates, the mean educational level of support staff is only 2.5 years less than for professional librarians.

Likes and Dislikes

The researchers also looked at staff likes and dislikes.[9] Respondents were asked, without prompting or precoded categories, what they like and what they dislike about their work. These responses were categorized only after all questionnaires were received. The findings, divided by professional status, are reported in Table 4.

A high proportion of both professional and support staff report liking technology. Use of the computer or technology is the third most frequently reported item by support staff, with 22.1 percent citing this as something they like. A liking for technology ranks lower for professional staff, but 12.4 percent of librarians also note use of the computer as one of the three things they like most about their job. Fewer than five percent of either group mention computers or technology as one of their three greatest dislikes. Added comments suggest that ergonomic issues (e.g., long hours at the terminal or eyestrain) were the most frequent sources of dislike. The other likes and dislikes are not directly related to technology use, but relate more broadly to working conditions and job content.

Both professionals and support staff report aspects of "independence and autonomy" most often when queried on their occupational likes (43.0 percent by professionals, 32.9 percent by support

TABLE 4. Responses and Frequencies for Professional and Support Staff to the Question: "What are the three things you like most about your job?"

	Professionals	Support Staff
independence, autonomy	43.0	32.9
working with patrons/public	25.8	18.8
coworkers, friendships with	23.7	24.2
working with certain collection /subject area	18.3	11.1
opportunity to try new ideas /creativity	16.7	14.8
supervising, directing, leading employees	16.1	10.1
intellectual stimulation	15.1	13.8
people (unspecified)	14.0	15.4
feeling of accomplishment /making a difference	14.0	5.4
variety	13.4	21.1
planning, policy-making	12.9	*
using the computer /working with technology	12.4	22.1
work atmosphere	7.5	13.4
benefits and atmosphere /opportunity for advancement	7.0	12.4
challenge	6.5	*
supervisor or quality of supervision	5.9	9.4
good work flow or organization	*	5.0
N	186	298

---

* Frequencies of less than 5 percent are not reported in light of the sample size.

staff). Typical replies found in both groups and collected under this heading include appreciating the ability to work free from supervision and approach tasks in the worker's preferred manner and flexibility afforded in time schedules. Professionals report liking work with the public more frequently than support staff (25.6 percent versus 18.8 percent), although on two other frequently offered responses — friendship with co-workers and people encountered in the workplace — both groups report similar preferences (23.7 and 14.0 percent among professionals, 24.2 and 15.4 percent among support staff). Other factors reflect consistency between the two groups. Both appreciate the opportunity for intellectual stimulation that a library offers (15.1 percent of professionals, 13.8 percent of support staff) and the opportunity for creative problem solving (16.7 percent of professionals, 14.8 percent of support staff). While 12.9 percent of professionals cite planning and policy-making as a satisfying activity, less than 5 percent of support staff do. This finding is expected and driven by the nature of organizations.

Support staff mention liking variety in work more often than professionals (21.4 percent compared to 13.4 percent). Professionals, with opportunities to develop special expertise or work in a subject area, may encounter or expect less variation in duties and responsibilities. Lack of variety does not necessarily reflect lack of substantively interesting work. A much higher percentage of professionals than support staff (14.0 percent vs. 5.4 percent) report "feeling of accomplishment or making a difference" as something they like about their work and 18.3 percent of professionals cite working with a certain collection or in a certain subject area. Many librarians enter the field with subject expertise or an affinity for certain disciplinary areas. They take up work as professionals because of the opportunities to work within those areas and increase specialization.

Both groups report a greater variety of dislikes about their jobs (see Table 5). In general, the responses to this question reveal more organizational or site specific dislikes, diluting the number of responses that could be aggregated meaningfully. Professionals report lack of time and the demands on time most frequently (25.3 percent), followed by "budget cuts and lack of funds" (22.0 percent). From comments offered during the focus group sessions, these

TABLE 5. Responses and Frequencies for Professional and Support Staff to the Question: "What are the three things you dislike most about your job?"

	Professionals	Support Staff
lack of time, workload too heavy	25.3	16.4
budget cuts, lack of funds	22.0	13.1
lack of challenge, too routine, repetitive	15.1	14.4
report writing /keeping statistics	14.0	11.4
personnel problems	13.4	18.1
library administration	11.8	8.1
doing supervising	11.8	7.1
environmental problems	9.7	10.4
committees, meetings	9.1	*
salary, pay	8.1	10.1
ambiguous chain of command	7.0	*
low image or status	6.5	7.4
supervisor problems	6.0	7.1
dealing with particular patrons or specific groups	*	7.4
lack of communication	*	6.4
tedious work	*	6.4
lack of opportunity for advancement	*	5.0
N	186	298

* Frequencies of less than 5 percent are not reported in light of the sample size.

items may be very much related. A number of staff discussed their heavy workload due to lack of staff and attribute the problem to budget cuts within the library or university.

Support staff cite these issues much less often (16.4 percent report lack of time, 13.1 percent cite budget cuts). Support staff report dislike of tedious work (6.4 percent) and the lack of opportunity for advancement (5.0 percent). Professionals are more likely to report a dislike for committees and meetings (9.1 percent) and for an ambiguous chain of command (7.0 percent). Fewer than five percent of support staff mention these problems.

The two groups are more similar in their disliking lack of challenge (15.1 percent for professionals, 14.4 percent for support staff), report writing (14.0 percent versus 11.4 percent), library administration (11.8 percent versus 8.1 percent), supervisor problems (6.0 percent versus 7.1 percent) and the office environment (9.7 percent versus 10.4 percent). The two groups are also similar in their level of dislike of "low image or low status of their jobs," but in this case it is probable support staff refer to their status in the organization while professionals may be concerned about both their organizational and professional status.

The categories into which these likes and dislikes fall are similar to patterns identified in Herzberg's (1959) studies of job satisfaction. As noted above, he correlates job satisfaction with aspects of the job itself; job dissatisfaction, with aspects of the job environment. Many of the things librarians like about their jobs relate to the work they do. Their dislikes more frequently relate to the workplace.

DISCUSSION

This study confirms many of the findings of previous job satisfaction investigations in the library labor force. Higher income, social interaction with colleagues and discretion over work have all been identified as possible or probable causes for satisfaction in prior studies. This study confirms Vaughn and Dunn's (1974) findings that institutional affiliation does not change the basic definition of what makes people happy on the job. Our findings indicate a stability in those factors which lead to job satisfaction dating as far back as Marchant's studies (1970, 1976). The importance of this similarity is that individual sources of job satisfaction appear to have remained constant at a time when the work is becoming increasingly automated.

It seems premature, however, to predict that technology use will have a neutral or positive effect in the future; for this study focuses on the individual, not the organization. It also occurs at a time when users are most likely to feel optimistic about implementation. Computerization of library processes often changes library procedures, client demand and workload. These changes affect the entire organization, including staff who spend little time themselves using computers, and may thus affect overall job satisfaction of the entire staff. Without research on overall satisfaction prior to and after automation, it is difficult to know how automation is affecting job satisfaction of those who spend little time with computers.

This study also occurs when computerization is still new for many staff. Attitudes are shaped by anticipation for and by lack of familiarity with this new tool. Technology can provide solutions to difficult problems and enable people to do things that could not be done before. As a librarian at one of the institutions studied said:

> I'm looking forward to [automated acquisitions] because I'm hoping that this system will help alleviate some problems we're dealing with right now. . . . I'm hoping it will be easier to keep track of and generate reports.

Some support staff report similar feelings:

> We had a bookkeeping machine when I first started. . . . The computer simplifies and makes it a lot easier to do what the old machine did. . . . My work has grown a lot too.

Statements in focus group discussions also reveal frustrations, and anxiety about new technologies. As one respondent notes:

> I feel a lot of frustration with the online catalog because we had this lovely little serials catalog where everything was right, and now we have to clean up lots of messes for the next few years. In the meantime we are on the firing line because

we're trying to explain all these messes and we can't get to them fast enough to please everyone.

Finally, throughout the 25 years that computer use has increased dramatically, the organizational structure of libraries and their use of personnel [with the exception perhaps of catalogers] have remained relatively stable. In these four libraries, and in most academic libraries, computers *substitute* for non-computerized processes; but only recently has their use begun to drive significant structural change in library organization.

Many changes are likely to occur in libraries in the next five to ten years. Librarians and support staff will use computers more extensively, integrated systems will change their relationship to library users and to one another, and the organizational structure of libraries may alter. Although these data cannot predict the future of job satisfaction in a technologically advanced library, they do suggest issues that should be considered in the application of technology. Workers' needs for control, independence and social interaction persist. Computer technology can easily diminish these when it is used partially as a tool for managerial control. As librarians restructure their organizations, they will want to explore how to design the work of both professional and support staff to meet the psychological and social needs of all their staff. As Zuboff (1988 p. 7) notes, the choices that we make about the use of technology will change the nature of authority in the workplace. And those choices will affect the psychological setting and feelings about work for those in the workplace.

NOTES

1. Mary D. Herrick, "Status of Worker Morale Among College Catalogers." *College and Research Libraries* 11 (January 1950): 18-32.
2. Evidence of this is given in the literature review reported in Harold D. Hosel, "Academic Librarians and Faculty Status – a Role Stress/Job Satisfaction Perspective," *Journal of Library Administration* 5 (Fall 1984): 57-66.
3. Herzberg's (1959) two-factor theory uses a technique in which the subject is prompted, through interviews with the investigator, to give descriptive examples of his or her own experiences of job satisfaction and dissatisfaction. The investigator later codes these descriptions on his or her own assessment of the

subject's situation. Authorities in the social sciences have questioned the integrity of this method and it has not been successfully replicated.

4. A number of other studies have also explored these types of relationships. Chwe (1976) employed the Minnesota Satisfaction Questionnaire to test whether reference librarians were more satisfied than catalogers. Chwe found statistically significant variation between these personnel on only three of the twenty dimensions tested, with overall satisfaction similar between the two groups.

Chrisman (1976) addressed the question of job satisfaction among catalogers using the Brayfield-Rothe Job Satisfaction Index. Chrisman found catalogers significantly less satisfied than their public service counterparts, although both groups scored above the mean in general level of satisfaction.

Several studies have sought to explain differences in satisfaction by demographic characteristics of the worker. In a study of 202 librarians from 23 academic libraries Wahba (1975) found women experienced lower levels of esteem and autonomy as a function of their work situation. Rockman (1984) returned to this question in a study which found the subject's sex to be related to job satisfaction, but it could not be used to predict overall satisfaction.

5. These four libraries were part of a larger study of 11 academic libraries. The names of the four libraries are not provided to preserve the confidentiality of the institutions.

6. The authors are indebted to William Form, Kaufman, and Toby Parcel (Department of Sociology, Ohio State University, Columbus, Ohio 43210-1353) for permission to modify and use their questionnaire.

7. At each library, a staff member coordinated the site visit by Estabrook. Prior to the visit all members of the professional, administrative and support staff (excluding student workers) received a letter from Estabrook that introduced the study as one about the relationship between technology and library work. Her letter was accompanied by a letter from the director or personnel officer of the participating library asking that all staff complete the questionnaire and providing them with information about the location and times for meetings. Estabrook administered questionnaires on-site to assure a sufficient response rate from participants.

8. For a list of the questions used in computing the variables, see the appendix.

9. This section of the study resembles an investigation of job stress and job satisfaction in the library conducted in stress management workshops between 1983 and 1986. Interested readers may wish to consult Charles Bunge, "Stress in the Library," *Library Journal* 112 (September 15, 1987): 47-51.

REFERENCES

Bengston, Dale Susan and Shields, Dorothy. "A Test of Marchant's Predictive Formulas Involving Job Satisfaction." *Journal of Academic Librarianship* 11 (May 1985): 88-92.

Blumberg, Marvin and Gerwin, Donald. "Coping with the Advanced Manufacturing Technology." (paper presented at the conference on The Quality of Work Life in the 80's) Toronto, August 30-September 3, 1981.

Braverman, Harry. *Labor and Monopoly Capital.* New York: Monthly Review Press, 1974.

Chrisman, Larry G. "Job Satisfaction and the Academic Library Cataloger." *Southeastern Librarian* 26 (Summer 1976): 69-83.

Chwe, Steven. "A Comparative Study of Librarians' Job Satisfaction: Catalogers and Reference Librarians in University Libraries." Ph.D. Dissertation, University of Pittsburgh, 1976.

D'Elia, George P. "The Determinants of Job Satisfaction Among Beginning Librarians." *Library Quarterly* 49 (July, 1979): 43-56.

Form, William H. "On the Degradation of Skills." *Annual Review of Sociology 1987* 13:29-47.

Hartmann, Heidi I., Kraut, Robert E., and Tilly, Luoise A., eds. *Computer Chips and Paper Clips: Technology and Women's Employment.* Washington, D.C.: National Academy Press, 1986.

Herrick, Mary D. "Status of Worker Morale Among College Catalogers," *College and Research Libraries* 11 (January 1950): 18-32.

Herzberg, Frederick. *The Motivation to Work.* New York: John Wiley, 1959.

Jones, Dorothy E. "Library Support Staff and Technology: Perceptions and Opinions." *Library Quarterly* 37 (Spring 1989): 432-56.

Lynch, Beverly P. and Verdin, JoAnn. "Job Satisfaction in Libraries: Relationships of the Work Itself, Age, Sex, Occupational Group, Tenure, Supervisory Level, Career Commitment and Library Department." *Library Quarterly* 53 (April 1983): 434-447.

Lynch, Beverly P. and Verdin, JoAnn. "Job Satisfaction in Libraries: A Replication." *Library Quarterly* 57 (April 1987): 190-202.

Marchant, Maurice P. "The Effects of the Decision-Making Process and Related Organizational Factors on Alternative Measures of Performance in University Libraries." Ph.D. Dissertation, University of Michigan, 1970.

Marchant, Maurice P. *Participative Management in Academic Libraries.* Westport, CT: Greenwood Press, 1976.

Plate, Kenneth H. and Stone, Elizabeth W. "Factors Affecting Librarians' Job Satisfaction: A Report of Two Studies." *Library Quarterly* 44 (April 1974): 97-110.

Pybril, Lawrence, "Job Satisfaction in Relation to Job Performance and Occupational Level." *Personnel Journal* 52 (1973): 94-100.

Noble, David. *Forces of Production.* New York: Alfred A. Knopf, 1984.

Rockman, Ilene F. "Job Satisfaction Among Faculty and Librarians: A Study of Gender, Autonomy and Decisionmaking Opportunities." *Journal of Library Administration* 5 (Fall 1984): 43-56.

Scammell, R.W. and Stead, B.A. "A Study of Age and Tenure as it Pertains to Job Satisfaction." *Journal of Library Administration* 1 (January 1980): 3-18.

Shaiken, Harley. *Work Transformed: Automation and Labor in the Computer Age*. New York: Holt, Rinehart, and Winston, 1985.

Vaughn, William J. and Dunn, J.D., "A Study of Job Satisfaction in Six University Libraries," *College and Research Libraries* 35 (May 1974): 163-177.

Wanba, Susanne Patterson. "Job Satisfaction of Librarians: A Comparison Between Men and Women." *College and Research Libraries* 36 (January 1975): 45-52.

Zuboff, Shoshana. *In the Age of the Smart Machine: the Future of Work and Power*. New York: Basic Books, 1988.

APPENDIX

Dependent Variable

Job Satisfaction

1) All things considered, how satisfied are you with your present job?

4=very satisfied; 3=somewhat satisfied; 2=a little satisfied; 1=not very satisfied

Independent Variables

Opportunity is the mean of responses to the following questions:

Indicate how likely each of the following statements is concerning your employment situation 2 years from now.

I will be making 20% more money than I am now.

I will have a job with substantially more responsibility than I have now.

I will have received at least one promotion at the library.

I will have skills that make me much more marketable than I am now.

I will have more managerial duties than I have now.

1= very unlikely, 2= somewhat unlikely, 3= somewhat likely, 4= very likely

Social Interaction is the mean of responses to the following questions:

APPENDIX (continued)

How frequently do you get together socially with other associates away from the job?

How frequently do you get together socially with your immediate supervisor away from the job?

How frequently do you eat lunch or spend your break time with associates who are part of your immediate section?

How frequently do you eat lunch or spend your break time with associates who are not part of your immediate section?

1= seldom or never, 2= several times a year, 3= once a month or more, 4= once a week or more, 5= almost every day

Discretion is the mean of responses on 4 questions:

For each of the following, indicate how often you do that kind of work.

follow a set way of doing one or two tasks?

follow a set way of doing many tasks?

1=always, 2=usually, 3=sometimes, 4=rarely, 5=never

adapt existing procedures to new tasks?

create new procedures for new tasks?

1=never, 2=usually, 3=sometimes, 4=rarely, 5=never

Job Stress is computed from the following two questions:

On a scale from 1 to 10, how much stress do you have in your life?

1   2   3   4   5   6   7   8   9   10
none   moderate   a great deal

What percentage of the stress in your life is job-related?

0%   10%   20%   30%   40%   50%   60%   70%   80%   90%   100%

The two responses are multiplied together to obtain job stress.

Performance Appraisal
in the Automated Environment

Geraldine B. King

The environment in which performance appraisal takes place in the late twentieth century library has changed in many significant and dramatic ways. The most obvious difference is the appearance of computer terminals. Library users who used to thumb through card catalogs or volumes of indexes and write out call numbers and citations with pencil and paper now read from screens and print screen copies. Check out occurs when the laser-scanner reads the users' and the items' bar codes. Reference librarians consult terminals at their reference desks which provide bibliographic access to the library's own materials, to interlibrary loan resources, and to thousands of journals. Those same terminals provide full-text access to many of the journals and other information databases.

All library workers' jobs have been affected by the new technology; in fact, "automation has revolutionized much of the day-to-day work of individual staff members" according to the A.L.A. publication *Library Administration and Management*.[1] But there is also an interaction between the technology, the individual job, and the structure or organization of the library which combines to have a more profound effect on one's performance, and therefore, affects performance appraisal.

According to Stanley Davis, author of *Future Perfect*, we have barely begun to see the effects of the service economy or the information age on the structures of our organizations.[2] Most of the orga-

Geraldine B. King is Associate Director of the Ramsey County Public Library, St. Paul, MN.

nizations in which we work are still based on the industrial model: a hierarchical or pyramid structure in which an employee reports to a supervisor who is responsible for seeing that the employee does what he/she's been told to do. Yet, for 30 to 35 years, Maslow, Herzberg, McGregor, and their followers have told us that the way to motivate employees is to give them greater individual responsibility and control over their own jobs, and provide opportunities for them to change, learn, and develop on the job. The impact of library automation on many library jobs has been to give greater responsibility and control over the task but not always with the needed authority, or with the recognition of the profound change by management.

More and more, work is accomplished by groups or teams working together rather than by individuals working in isolation. The work of individuals which was related to the work of others through the supervisor or manager may now often be connected by the computer. Some libraries are moving toward structural and organizational changes that reflect the changes in management theory and the impact of technology. Forerunners of tomorrow's possible organizational models include networks, matrix management, a holistic approach emphasizing the customer-employee relationship, boundary-spanning theory, and horizontal management.

What effect is all this having on performance appraisal?

Of all the functions of personnel management, there seems to be more dissatisfaction with performance appraisal than any other. More is probably written about it than any other function; yet it remains an unresolved problem and one of perpetual interest. Everyone thinks "there must be a better way to do it than we do it here."[3] Nothing less than a complete overhaul of the philosophy and rationale of performance appraisal will result in a system that fits the automated library in the service economy/information age.

However, many libraries are required to use a generic system or form prescribed by the jurisdiction or institution of which they are a part — a system which often gives the impression that it must have been designed for some other part of the university or county or city. Nevertheless, it may be possible to substitute a scheme which is more helpful, or to expand on the existing system, or adapt it more specifically to the library's needs. Minimal effort can be devoted to the required form or system, thus releasing staff time to design and develop a performance appraisal system which is a good fit for the specific library. Such a system can be a framework for the overall management of performance.

While developing a unique system may seem a formidable undertaking, if taken one step at a time, using available resources, it can be done and will prove well worth the effort. As more library-specific systems are developed, there are more resources available to help other libraries develop their own systems. For example, as one library develops well-written, clear behavioral statements for specific performance standards for reference work, the next library's task is easier. Or, as competency lists are developed in several projects for automated circulation desk work, those lists can be adapted to other libraries.

STEPS IN DEVELOPING A PERFORMANCE APPRAISAL SYSTEM TO FIT A SPECIFIC LIBRARY

The first step in developing a unique performance appraisal system is to think through the objectives and criteria.

- What *must* the performance appraisal system do?
- What do you *want* it to do?

Perhaps the question with the broadest implications for designing a performance appraisal system is whether it is needed to rate/grade employees on a comparative basis to distribute pay. While "pay for performance" is somewhat more common in industrial and business settings, many libraries do not have to consider this objective and can design a system which focuses on the individual's development rather than the administration of the library.

It is possible to take a system that is designed as a self-rating developmental system and use that same rating system for the designated "raters" (supervisor, peers, etc.) to assign comparative ratings to employees, or to adapt it so that clients (e.g., students) may rate librarians.

A more positive approach is to look at rating as a longitudinal comparison of the individual's development over time. A necessary result of such a performance appraisal is a personal development plan tied to the knowledge and skills needed to do the present job. A related desirable criterion would be a long-range development plan geared to a position to which the individual might aspire or to the person's career goals.

Other criteria which a specific performance appraisal system might require is an objective writing and appraisal system tied to departmental and library-wide objectives and goals.

Finally, an essential criterion is some way to match the individual's setting of priorities and those of the department (the peer group) and the library as a whole.

Desirable criteria might include the opportunity to discuss problem areas with colleagues and receive suggestions and help from them—a kind of brainstorming session centered on the individual's duties. A related objective of such a performance appraisal system might be team building. A group discussion would also cover areas in which the duties of the employee being evaluated might be duties shared or worked on together by other members of the group.

Another desirable criterion of a performance appraisal system would be some way of including the effect on the performance of factors over which the employee has no control. Probably the most common example is increased usage, meaning more time spent in direct public service and less time for accomplishing indirect tasks such as collection development.

Another decision which needs to be made about the proposed performance appraisal system is who will be doing the appraising. Supervisor, self, peer group, supervisees, and users are all individuals or groups which need to be considered as possible sources of input. Each subdivision of a library staff will need to decide which individuals or groups are relevant to the appraisal of their unit's work.

Once a clear set of objectives for the unique performance appraisal system has been decided upon, the next step is to translate those objectives into the component parts of the process itself.

COMPONENTS OF A PERFORMANCE APPRAISAL SYSTEM

Components which should be considered are:

a. behavioral performance standards, or competencies: attitudes, knowledge, skills (e.g., what a reference librarian needs to know or be able to do in order to find the information requested by the library user);
b. factors, other than personal competencies, which affect the individual's ability to do the job (e.g., budget);
c. the individual's objectives—both those just completed and those proposed for the next time period;
d. the individual's current specific task assignments, in the priority order understood by the individual; and
e. career goals, long range objectives.

The most time-consuming part of the initial design of a system is the preparing of the detailed description of the job itself: the knowledge, skills, and attitudes needed. This may become a competency checklist, a series of behavioral descriptions of various job factors, or a description of performance standards. Many performance appraisal systems fail at this point because the effort is not put into individually tailored descriptions. A system based on a list of management factors needed for a generic management job in a hierarchical structure is just not good enough. It addresses neither the uniqueness of the library as a workplace nor the skills needed for successful management now and in the future. Equally inadequate is a listing of skills prepared for a non-automated library.

Automation has required library workers to develop and use skills which they never anticipated needing when they entered the library workplace. Public service librarians need a sufficiently detailed knowledge of MARC to understand what is included in the various indexes in online catalogs. They need skills in teaching basic computer literacy; they often must perform the very first introduction to computer use for many of their patrons.

Circulation desk assistants should have greater individual responsibility for dealing with the library user's problem, should be far more knowledgeable about library policies, and should be able to manipulate the intricacies of the computer system. They are freed from the need for many basic clerical skills, but instead need higher levels of interpersonal skills. They must continuously make decisions and exercise judgement on the front line.

Some libraries have prepared and various research studies have provided lists of competencies or behavioral performance descriptions for library work. There is material covering reference, technical services, aspects of library management, and even some computer skills. There are lists specifically aimed at academic or public libraries, and at large or small libraries. While some of the available materials are over ten years old, it is still time-saving to start with established lists and then add, subtract, or modify, to fit the specific library, individual job, and new technology and services.

The preparation of a list for a specific job or individual would include the following steps: first, compiling all the relevant resource lists that can be found; second, eliminating duplication and identifying gaps; third, editing the remaining materials and writing new material to prepare a draft; and fourth, evaluating the draft by all who will be involved in its use.

Once all have agreed upon a draft, they should rank competencies as essential, desirable and moderately important. Or, if behavioral performance standards are being written, scaled descriptions should be agreed upon by all participating in the process. Thus, a final "ranked" list for appraisal use is prepared.

While preparing the list is time-consuming, it is a valuable experience to write an agreed upon detailed description of the job; misunderstandings will be discussed and resolved in the process, and much clarity of communication will result. Subsequent use of the list requires far less staff preparation time; the only necessity is to monitor for the inclusion of new technology, and new or modified services.

In addition to the personal competencies or performance standards which are needed to evaluate performance, there are other factors which affect the individual's capability to perform, but over which the individual has no control — extrinsic job factors. Primary reasons for unsuccessful performance or failure to meet objectives may be extrinsic. An easily understood example is the task or project dependent on a specific budget appropriation which is not received. Other needed resources, such as equipment, space, etc., may not be available. Unanticipated environmental situations can impinge on performance — everything from burned-out air-conditioner compressors on hot humid days to major remodeling projects. In the automated library, there is the dreaded "system down." Patrons easily raise their expectations of service from an automated library. When they become accustomed to having their document availability problems solved "on the spot" by circulation clerks who have all the information from the automated systems available on their terminal, they are less than pleased when told they will have to wait. Such stressful interactions with patrons can have a detrimental effect on overall performance.

Team projects may fail because of problems with the performance of other members of the group. Work group conflict or problems with collegial decision making may affect the individual's ability to complete his/her part of the task. Leadership in the group may be inadequate to the task. Factors in the structure of the overall organization — the size and complexity, type of organization, management styles, climate or organizational culture — also affect the individual's ability to do his/her job.

Networks and interlibrary cooperation are also factors which should be taken into consideration. Inability to provide interlibrary loan items for a patron may be the result of the lending library's policies. The clientele of the library certainly affects the individual employee's performance and should be taken into account in evaluation. For example, the reactions of different users to learning the techniques of searching an automated public access catalog vary from excitement and eagerness to fear.

In addition to the needed knowledge, skills, and attitudes, other personal factors which can affect job performance are physical health and psychological factors including over-all job satisfaction, "burn-out," "plateauing," and perception of recognition and rewards. The ease with which an automated system provides supervisory monitoring of an individual's work may result in a feeling of lack of freedom and authority.[4]

A third part of a performance appraisal system is evaluation based on the current work assignment of the individual as expressed in individual objectives. Accomplishment or handling of objectives during the time since the previous appraisal needs to be evaluated. The individual's draft objectives for the next evaluation period should be discussed and modifications resulting from the performance appraisal, the work unit's objectives, and other team members' objectives should be made. Addressing needs for improvement and personal development in objectives for future implementation is particularly essential.

In order to evaluate and rank competencies and personal objectives, the individual's current work task assignments must be the framework within which the performance appraisal is done. In a supervisor-supervisee situation, both persons are reasonably aware of the individual's specific responsibilities although a review of them ensures that both are discussing from the same understanding. This process can be a check on agreement of priorities.

In a peer group evaluation, clarification of work assignments is particularly essential. Various co-workers will be more or less familiar with some parts of each individual's duties, but may be completely unaware of others and not have a total picture in perspective.

A final component in a performance management system is the career development of the individual: what future plans, career goals, or five-year goals does the individual have? As the field of career planning and development becomes more sophisticated with many more alternatives than just "getting ahead" to be considered, this becomes a more significant part of the performance appraisal process.[5]

Finally, in developing a specific unique performance appraisal system, a program for training those who will use the system is an important component part. The training should include material on the theory of performance management and the techniques needed to implement the system such as competency and objective writing, discussion methods, questioning skills, listening techniques, and dealing with confrontation.

EVALUATION OF A PERFORMANCE APPRAISAL SYSTEM

A performance appraisal system must be judged by the ongoing communication which it engenders and encourages. Performance management is not a once-a-year formal process but a day-in day-out coordination of staff and tasks. A successful performance appraisal system can help set library, work unit, and individual objectives and priorities; increase trust among colleagues and enhance team development; encourage problem-solving discussion and group decision-making; increase morale and job satisfaction; and assist the individual in career development.

FUTURE TRENDS IN PERFORMANCE APPRAISAL

Performance appraisal in the future will need to be suited to a better educated work force with individuals who have clearer ideas about their own career development, what they want to achieve and to learn on the job, and how they want to balance work and non-work activities. The systems will be evaluated by their usefulness to all parties involved—administrators, supervisors, colleagues, teams, employees, clients—rather than solely for their use for administrative purposes. Thus, there will be increasing emphasis on self-appraisal combined with multiple evaluation of the individual.[6] Library management which does not promote the development of a system which fits their unique environment will be sending a message to their employees that will result in less effective library service.

NOTES

1. "Why Is It That . . .," *Library Administration and Management* 3 (Spring 1989):56.
2. Stanley Davis, *Future Perfect* (Reading, Mass.: Addison-Wesley, 1987), p. 5.

3. Geraldine King, ed., *T.I.P. Kit No. 11: Managing Employee Performance* (Chicago: ALA Office of Library Personnel Resources, 1988).

4. Debora Shaw, ed., *Human Aspects of Library Automation: Helping Staff and Patrons Cope*. 1985 Clinic on Library Applications of Data Processing (Urbana-Champaign, Ill.: University of Illinois Graduate School of Library and Information Science, 1986).

5. C. Brooklyn Derr, *Managing the New Careerists* (San Francisco: Jossey-Bass, 1986).

6. Clive Fletcher and Richard Williams, *Performance Appraisal and Career Development* (London: Hutchinson, 1985).

Library Automation and Personnel Issues: A Selected Bibliography

Margaret Myers

Andrews, Virginia Lee, and Kelley, Carol Marie. "Changing Staffing Patterns in Technical Services Since the 1970s: A Study in Change." *Journal of Library Administration* 9, no. 1 (1988); 55-70.

Changes in library assistant workflow at the Texas Tech University are described, along with training plans as the assistants faced increasing responsibilities.

Atkinson, Hugh C. "The Impact of New Technology on Library Organization." *The Bowker Annual of Library and Book Trade Information*. 29th ed. New York: R. R. Bowker, 1984, pp. 109-114.

Changes in organizational structure as a result of automation, including decentralization and its effect on administration, may evolve even further with the advent of newer and different technologies.

Association of Research Libraries. Office of Management Studies. *Automation and Reorganization of Technical and Public Services*. SPEC Kit 112. Washington, D.C.: ARL, 1984.

Survey of 82 ARL libraries reports some integration of technical and public services, but none with complete integration.

Margaret Myers is Director, Office for Library Personnel Resources, American Library Association, Chicago, IL.

_____. *Managing Copy Cataloging in ARL Libraries*. SPEC Kit 136. Washington, D.C.: ARL, 1987.

Workflow, priorities, performance standards, and training are changing as a result of technological advances.

_____. *Staff Training for Automation in ARL Libraries*. SPEC Kit 109. Washington, D.C.: ARL, 1984.

A variety of methods are used in ARL libraries for staff development when automation takes place.

_____. *Systems Office Organization*. SPEC Kit 128. Washington, D.C.: ARL, 1986.

Organizational structures for systems personnel show various patterns in staffing, workflow, and location within the library.

Boyce, Bert R., and Heim, Kathleen M. "The Education of Library Systems Analysts for the Nineties." *Journal of Library Administration* 9, no. 4 (1988): 69-76.

Schools of library and information science will be hard-pressed to supply graduates with appropriate skills. Information literacy prior to matriculation will be more necessary.

Buck, Dayna. "Bringing Up an Automated Circulation System: Staffing Needs." *Wilson Library Bulletin* 60 (March 1986); 28-31.

Results of a staffing survey sent to Geac installations in libraries. Three-quarters had made changes to organizational chart because of automation.

Clinic on Library Applications of Data Processing. (Papers presented at the 22nd Annual Clinic on Library Applications of Data Processing, April 14-16, 1985.) *Human Aspects of Library Automation: Helping Staff and Patrons Cope*. Edited by Debora Shaw. Urbana-Champaign, Ill.: University of Illinois Graduate School of Library and Information Science, 1986.

Papers deal with training, ergonomics, planning, staff involvement and effects of technological change.

_____. (Papers presented at the 20th Annual Clinic on Library Applications of Data Processing, April 24-26, 1983.) *Professional Competencies-Technology and the Librarian.* Edited by Linda C. Smith. Urbana-Champaign, Ill.: University of Illinois Graduate School of Library and Information Science, 1988.

Papers deal with the changing roles and responsibilities of a variety of librarian positions.

Cochrane, Pauline A. "The Changing Roles and Relationships of Staff in Technical Services and Reference/Readers' Services in the Era of Online Public Access Catalogs." *The Reference Librarian* 9 (Fall/Winter 1988): 51-53.

The online catalog needs to be fashioned by a collaborative effort between public and technical services librarians.

Corbin, John. "The Education of Librarians in an Age of Information Technology." *Journal of Library Administration* 9, no. 1 (1988): 77-87.

Joint efforts of schools of library and information sciences and the libraries employing librarians need to be undertaken to ensure a planned continuum of lifelong education.

_____. *Implementing the Automated Library System.* Phoenix; Oryx, 1988.

Included are chapters on organizational and management structure, tasks and procedures, job design and staffing.

Creth, Sheila D. *Effective On-the-Job Training.* Chicago: American Library Association, 1986.

As part of an overall guidebook, Creth describes training in the electronic library. There will be new considerations and supervisors will find training more demanding and difficult.

Dakshinamurti, Ganga. "Automation's Effect on Library Personnel." *Canadian Library Journal* 42 (December 1985); 343-351.

Survey data on reactions of library personnel towards library automation are presented.

Daly, Jay. *Staff Personality Problems in the Library Automation Process*. Littleton, Colo.: Libraries Unlimited, 1985.

Five case studies introduce staff issues involved with implementing automation.

Das Gupta, Krishna. "The Impact of Technology on the Role of the Technical Services Librarian of Academia in the USA." *International Library Review* 13 (October 1981): 397-408.

Fifty academic libraries in New England were surveyed on trends in the general workflow of technical services departments.

Fayen, Emily Gallup. "Beyond Technology: Rethinking 'Librarian'." *American Libraries* 17 (April 1986); 240-242.

Technology provides an opportunity to redefine the role of librarians and have their services more valued. Suggestions are made to provide the best, most timely information similar to services carried out by corporation database managers.

Foster, Constance L. "Staff Considerations in Technical Services: The Chameleon Approach." *Journal of Library Administration* 9, no. 1 (1988): 71-86.

Organizational changes due to automation include restructuring positions, job training, ergonomics, and increased communication needs.

Freedman, Maurice J. "Automation and the Future of Technical Services." *Library Journal* 109 (June 15, 1984): 1197-1203.

Changing responsibilities and assignments of professional and paraprofessional staff are discussed, along with the kinds of departmental reorganization which may be necessary.

Getz, Malcolm, and Phelps, Doug. "Labor Costs in the Technical Operation of Three Research Libraries." *Journal of Academic Librarianship* 10 (September 1984): 209-219.

Technical services costs vary greatly among research libraries, but differences in costs do not appear to arise from differences in automation.

Glogoff, Louise Garraux; Dean, Barbara C.; and Highsmith, Anne
L. "Computer-Based Training for Cataloging Department Staff."
Journal of Academic Librarianship 10 (March 1984); 23-28.

A variety of techniques, including computer technology, have
been used by Pennsylvania State University Libraries to increase
the efficiency of training cataloging staff.

Gorman, Michael. "The Ecumenical Library." *The Reference Librarian* 9 (Fall/Winter 1983): 55-64.

A model for reorganization of library staff in an automated library is outlined.

Hafter, Ruth. *Academic Libraries and Cataloging Networks: Visibility, Control, and Professional Status*. Westport, Conn.:
Greenwood Press, 1986.

Library dependence upon online networks forces reevaluation of
traditional professional activities and the standards upon which
these are based.

Hill, Janet Swan. "Staffing Technical Services in 1995." *Journal
of Library Administration* 9, no. 1 (1988): 87-103.

The nature of changing technical services work is explored. Education and recruitment are crucial since technical services remains labor intensive regardless of widespread automation.

Hobert, Collin B., and Morris, Dilye C. "Cataloging and Searching Combined." *Journal of Academic Librarianship* 10 (March
1984): 10-16.

Reorganization of monographic processing staff at Iowa State
University Library has resulted in a highly efficient and speedy
system.

Horny, Karen L. "Fifteen Years of Automation: Evolution of Technical Services Staffing." *Library Resources and Technical Services* 31 (January/March 1987): 69-76.

Northwestern University Library's automation has resulted in economies from staffing reductions, plus enhanced service and increased quality of work.

————. "Managing Change: Technology and the Profession." *Library Journal* 110 (October 1, 1985): 56-58.

Library decentralization and higher levels of knowledge and skill of support staff are two aspects of change with automation.

————. "Where Do You Draw the Line? Changing Responsibilities in the Automated Environment." *Connecticut Libraries* 30 (July/August 1988): 1, 7-11.

The true nature of work may remain the same, but perceptions of it have been altered by applications of the new technology. Staff jobs require more attention to detail and ability to work with a complex system.

Hurych, Jitka. "The Professional and the Client: The Reference Interview Revisited." In *Video to Online: Reference Services and the New Technology*, edited by Bill Katz and Ruth A. Fraley. New York: Haworth Press, 1988, pp. 199-205.

Some changes in the reference interview occur because of online information services.

Johnson, Peggy. "Implementing Technological Change." *College and Research Libraries* 49 (January 1988): 38-46.

An understanding of organizational behavior is important in designing strategies for introducing technology. Recognizing contributions of library staff is central.

Kirkland, Janice J., ed. "Human Response to Library Automation." *Library Trends* 37 (Spring 1989): whole issue.

Topics include role of nonlibrarian automation specialists, divisions between library departments, satisfaction and quality of worklife, and options for moderating staff stress levels.

Kratz, Charles, ed. *Training Issues in Changing Technology*. Chicago: American Library Association, 1986.

Prepared by the ALA Library Administration and Management Association's Personnel Administration Section, the nine essays address ergonomics, change, using technology to train, and human factors in adopting library technology.

Kritz, Harry M., and Kok, Victoria K. "The Computerized Reference Department: Buying the Future." *RQ* 25 (Winter 1985): 198-203.

Systematic computerization of reference and collection management functions at Virginia Polytechnic have resulted in increased effectiveness and productivity of library staff.

Lynch, Beverly P. "Changes in Library Organization." In *Leadership for Research Libraries: A Festschrift for Robert M. Hayes*, pp. 67-78. Edited by Anne Woodsworth and Barbara von Wahlde. Metuchen, N.J.: Scarecrow Press, 1988.

Libraries are seeking new structures to accommodate the impact of technology. They are reconfiguring departmental and work designs in terms of decision-making structures for the coordination of work flow and information flows.

Martin, Susan K. "The Role of the Systems Librarian." *Journal of Library Administration* 9, no. 4 (1988): 57-76.

Responsibilities of systems librarians are outlined, along with organizational placement of this specialist position and qualifications for this type of person.

McKinley, Margaret. "Serials Staffing Guidelines for the 80s." In *The Serials Collection: Organization and Administration*, edited by Nancy Jean Melin. Ann Arbor, Mich.: Pierian Press, 1982.

Suggestions for minimizing the negative aspects and increasing positive benefits of automation are presented. Called for is a management approach which stresses flexibility.

Miller, Inabeth. "Technology: Staff Issues." In *Microcomputers in Libraries*, edited by Ching-chih Chen and Stacey E. Bressler. New York: Neal-Schuman, 1982, pp. 157-167.

Various models of staff training in technology are reviewed.

Nichols, Elizabeth Dickinson. "Changing Roles, Changing Job Descriptions in Technical Services." *Library Personnel News* 2 (Winter 1988): 5-6.

Changes in professional and paraprofessional roles due to automation at the Stockton-San Joaquin County Public Library are addressed.

Nielsen, Brian. "An Unfolding, Not an Unveiling: Creating an Online Public Library." *Library Journal* 109 (June 15, 1984): 1215-1218.

Involvement of the total library staff in the process of developing an online catalog is necessary to produce satisfactory results.

_____. "Online Bibliographic Searching and the Deprofessionalization of Librarianship." *Online Review* 4 (September 1980): 218-223.

Explored is the debate over whether or not technological change increases or decreases the professional status of librarians.

Olsgaard, John N. "Automation as a Socio-Organizational Agent of Change: An Evaluative Literature Review." *Information Technology and Libraries* 4 (March 1985): 19-20.

Organizational and behavioral or human problems in introducing computer-based systems are reviewed.

Preston, Gregor A. "How Will Automation Affect Cataloging Staff?" *Technical Services Quarterly* 1 (Fall/Winter 1983): 129-136.

Predictions are made regarding the future in technical services departments in a fully automated setting.

Rhine, Leonard. "Effects of the Adoption of an Integrated Online System on a Technical Services Department." *Library Hi Tech* 16 (Winter 1986): 89-92.

University of Florida Health Science Center Library Staff were surveyed to evaluate work setting changes and intangible changes because of automation. Positive benefits were noted in productivity and attitudes; negative comments related mostly to physical aspects.

Richards, Timothy F. "The Online Catalog: Issues in Planning and Development." *Journal of Academic Librarianship* 10 (March 1984): 4-9.

Introduction of an online catalog will have an impact on library staff, in terms of organizational structure, productivity, and type of work.

Rooks, Dana C., and Thompson, Linda L. "Impact of Automation on Technical Services," *Journal of Library Administration* 9, no. 1 (1988): 121-136.

Both individual job-related considerations and organizational implications need to be addressed.

Sievert, Mary Ellen; Albritton, Rosie L.; Roper, Paula; and Clayton, Nina. "Investigating Computer Anxiety in an Academic Library." *Information Technology and Libraries* 7 (September 1988): 243-252.

Determinants of computer anxiety were studied with participants at the University of Missouri-Columbia Libraries. They were influenced by their previous computer experience, their departments, and the number of years worked in the library.

Sorensen, Borge. "Library Automation—Its Impact on Library Service, Working Conditions and Employment." *Scandinavian Public Library Quarterly* 16, no. 1 (1983): 8-13.

Concerns raised by Danish trade unions about automation in libraries might have some application to U.S. situations.

Surprenant, Thomas T., and Perry-Holmes, Claudia. "The Reference Librarians of the Future: A Scenario." *RQ* 25 (Winter 1985): 234-238.

The organization of the reference function will change, with the librarian acting much like an individual entrepreneur.

Urbanek, Val. "Staff Training and Automation: Issues and Concerns for Library Managers." In *Microcomputers in Libraries*, edited by Ching-chih Chen and Stacey E. Bressler. New York: Neal-Schuman, 1982, pp. 157-167.

Practical guidelines for addressing staff needs during introduction of any automation project are presented.

Webb, T. D. *The In-House Option: Professional Issues of Library Automation*. New York, Haworth, 1987.

Computer skills required of systems staff and how library education can best provide technological skills in the future are addressed.

White, Herbert S. *Library Personnel Management*. White Plains, N.Y.: Knowledge Industry, 1985.

A chapter on adapting to changes in technology is part of this overall personnel manual.

Printed in the United States
by Baker & Taylor Publisher Services